NURSE PAPA

NURSE PAPA

16 MEDITATIONS ON PARENTHOOD
FROM A PEDIATRIC ONCOLOGY NURSE

DAVID METZGER R.N.

GenZ
The Future of Publishing

ISBN (Paperback): 978-1-952919-49-7
ISBN (eBook): 978-1-952919-50-3

GenZPublishing.org

Aberdeen, NJ

This book would not have been possible if not for the support of my wife and the inspiration of my children. Kaveena, you are my first and best editor. Thank you for putting up with my obsession and for being so very generous with your love. Szivika and Dayus, every moment with you both is a joy and an education. Being your papa is the greatest gift I have ever received.

Nurse Papa is also a popular podcast. In each episode the author takes a deep dive into stories of parenthood and comes out on the other side with a better understanding of what makes kids and parents tick. You will laugh, you will cry, and you will learn more about yourself with each episode. Click away and please enjoy this immersive audio experience along with the book.

AUTHOR'S NOTE

I am not an expert in parenting. In fact, I often feel lost, overwhelmed, and wildly unequipped for the daily task of rearing my own children. So, if you are seeking tips concerning the nitty-gritties of raising kids—tricks for getting them to bed, ways to limit their screen time, or helpful persuasions for them to eat green things—you will not find them here. You will discover something else though; something deeper and more elusive. You will learn what it truly means to raise children—the joys, the pains, the fears, the many failures, and sometimes, the triumphs.

This book is a meditation on what it means to be a caregiver to children, both sick and healthy, in our complicated world; an emotional guide of sorts. My work as a nurse to sick and dying children has given me insight into how to be the kind of father I strive to be. It has forever altered my role as a parent. As I have taken care of these sick children and their parents in the hospital, they have shared the most intimate parts of their lives with me, and I have done the same in return. Through their care and their love, they have shown me what it means to live well and, far too often, what it means to die well. This book is for them.

In *Nurse Papa*, you will learn from the experiences and reflections of many different people (nurses, doctors, the patients, and their parents), but this book is not meant to be read as a linear narrative. You might be introduced to a character in a particular chapter and not hear from them again afterward. The thoughts and feelings of other people reappear numerous times throughout the book. Each perspective is unique and meant to illuminate the meditations on parenthood that I have discovered.

Although these meditations are sincere and often profound, the serious context in which they are described may make them challenging to take in. For this reason, I have made an effort to include funny, sometimes even silly, pauses between these meditations. These interludes, titled "Breaks From the Heartbreak," reveal unexpectedly humorous aspects of the home and hospital experience. They remind the reader that levity exists here too, and that great insight can be derived from both sorrow and happiness.

The events described in this book are based on my experiences as a nurse and as a parent. With the exception of those who have granted explicit permission to use their names and descriptions, the identifying features of people and places have been changed in order to protect the privacy of my patients and colleagues. Descriptions of certain individuals and situations have been altered to further protect identities.

TABLE OF CONTENTS

A LETTER TO MY BABY

Baby,
when you finally arrive here
you may find
a world more dusty
and dangerous
than offered by your former, more cushy quarters.

Your caretakers, too—these "parents"
may appear less seaworthy than you would prefer
for this voyage of raising a child
but nobody else showed up to claim you

So, there you have it.

Rest assured, kiddo,
despite all their baggage and wrinkles,
these two people will float right alongside you
under the power of your wind and the pull of your tides

They will show you what they know of this world
how to laugh, how to cry, and to love,
how to give, how to take, and to hope

and

just maybe,

you will listen to some of it

PROLOGUE
That Kid Look

These kids were totally different kids before. They were once healthy and running around. Once, they had an entire life, of friends, of things they loved to do. We don't get to see that.

— Amy, pediatric oncology nurse, mother

The long hallway of this hospital unit follows an elongated horseshoe pattern, with all of the patient rooms oriented on the outside. These rooms have large windows and a striking view of the San Francisco Bay. When the light of the sun is allowed to pour in, the rooms feel airy and open. When the drapes are drawn shut and the overhead lights turned off though, each room can be as cool and dark as the cave of a snoozing bear.

Some patients prefer their space dim and silent as they sleep their way through indeterminate stays. Sleep can be preferable to the other states available to them: nausea, pain, boredom, or all three simultaneously. But there are other patients who seek the stimulus of the world on the other side of the glass. They spend their days sitting on the ledge beneath the large bay windows, their noses and hands pressed against it, smudgy marks left behind. They play with their parents and siblings, scribble at homework that not even cancer can help them escape from, or watch movies on the big-screen television that seems almost as large as a studio apartment I once lived in.

Outside these patient rooms, nurses in royal-blue scrubs, doctors in their street clothes with stethoscopes hanging around their necks, and various other hospital staff in green, grey, and light-blue uniforms roam up and down the halls. The drum of their conversations, the beeping of monitors, and the occasional blare of overhead announcements ensure a steady white noise that most who work here hardly notice anymore. Visitors unfamiliar with the long layout often find themselves fully circumnavigating the entire horseshoe shape before they find the exit, which is also the entrance.

Of the long line of identical doors spaced evenly along the hallway of this pediatric oncology ward, most were shut. The sounds of sick children and their families distilled indecipherably out into the hallway.

The room I was standing near was silent though, the inhabitants within saddened and struck mute. The girl inside who once laughed, cried, endured, and grew bored in this room and others just like it, died early in the morning. Her name was Lucia. I remember her cute chubby face and the tight curls of her brown hair, before it all fell out. She once wore the same flowery red dress for days in a row despite her mom's ardent protests. Her large family sat around the bed where her body lay, sometimes speaking in hushed tones, but mostly just sitting. She was wearing that same red dress. It had thin shoulder straps. The small patterned flowers were blue and yellow.

Veronica, Lucia's younger sister, could not be easily contained to a silent room. A shorter and plumper doppelganger of Lucia, she was happily playing with a small inflatable ball just outside the door, bouncing it against a wall and singing softly to herself.

I first met Lucia a year or so before she died. I was a new nurse then, still walking those hallways in confused circles myself. She was a newly diagnosed cancer patient. Leukemia. The first night I took care of her, I was working with a nurse who was training me. Lucia was sick and feverish, shivering in her bed. We had to wake her shortly after midnight to draw blood from her already-bruised body to determine how we would treat her. Her sleepy eyes were wide and fearful of the advancing needle that I held. My hand was shaking with nervousness, while her hand—my tiny target—was strangely still. If they were interested, the bookies in Vegas would have offered equal odds over who was more scared in that moment, me or the prepubescent girl from whose body I was about to draw blood. Rivulets of sweat dripped from my brow as I pushed the needle into her skin and connected to her vein.

Still standing outside the door where Lucia's body lay, I was shaken from this memory by the phone buzzing in my pocket. When I answered it, I heard the muffled request of a mother asking for medication for her vomiting son. As I walked quickly to help them, I made sure to end the call from the boy's room. I once forgot to do this before placing my phone back into the front pocket of my scrubs, and the young girl and her mother were treated to the unmistakable sounds of a grown man using the restroom.

I passed by an open door. Inside was a bored teenage girl. She was lying in bed and watching television. Her skin was pale. Her smooth head was covered by a beanie that her mom had knitted at her bedside. A catheter exited at a point on the right of her chest and connected to a tangle of clear plastic tubes that led to a humming medication pump next to her bed. A tray of untouched food sat ignored in front of her. She waved and smiled as I passed by.

The next door over was closed. I could hear a loud yell from the child within, but it was not clear to me if it was a laugh or a cry. Here, where the expression of every possible human emotion is not only accepted, but expected, it can sometimes be difficult to distinguish between the two.

Just before I entered the room to which I had been summoned (I could hear the boy retching and coughing inside), I noticed

Veronica, Lucia's look-alike sister, next to me. She had migrated down the hall while I was lost in the memory of her older sibling. She was still playfully distracted in her own little world. Veronica was quite used to this place by now—a veritable sibling appendage. The bouncing ball had escaped from her grasp and she was chasing after it, away from the hospital room where her sister's body, still in that red dress, lay. As she skipped down the hallway, her arms stretched out in front of her, she sang loudly enough for me to hear her words. The tune was some variation of a common nursery rhyme, but the words were all her own.

"My sister is an angel, my sister is an angel, my sister is an angel, my sister is an angel," she sang between giggles. Clearly, one of her family members had tried to explain Lucia's death in a way that a young child might understand. Her refrain reminded me of a scratched record, upon which the needle was not merely stuck, but almost willing itself into action. The ball she had been chasing came to rest against the side of the hallway. Pausing in her song, Veronica stared at me with a blank kid expression that seemed to convey neither trust nor suspicion, but rather some emotion in between. It puzzled me at the time.

Now, years later, with over a decade of pediatric nursing and six years of child-rearing under my belt, it is a look I have come to know all too well. It is the same faraway glance that my precocious six-year-old daughter routinely drops on me when she possesses neither the words, desire, nor patience to tell me what is really on her mind. I wanted to say something meaningful to this girl with a newly dead sister, something that would explain why this was all happening, but I had no good explanation for it. Only useless platitudes came to my mind.

Ignoring me fully, she began her refrain again. This time, it was only a hum, but her words stayed with me. My sister is an angel. My sister is an angel. My sister is an angel. My sister is an angel. Then, for no apparent reason, the skipping record in Veronica's mind stopped. She picked up her ball and headed back in the direction from which she had come.

CARING FOR CHILDREN
The Beginning

I left work crying on my first day. I thought that there is no way that I can do this. What the hell have I done?

- Cassi, pediatric oncology nurse, mother

When I told my sweet, yet admittedly salty grandmother that I wanted to go to nursing school, I was worried how she might respond. She was old-fashioned and her talk was always straight. I chose to tell her in a setting in which her defenses would be down: a Palm Springs buffet restaurant filled primarily with octogenarians eating their requisite five o'clock dinners.

As my grandmother slyly absconded with bread rolls, which would find a permanent home in her freezer, I hoped she would be too distracted to think much of my new career revelation. The ploy did not work. Upon hearing my plan, she looked at me with a startled expression in her watery sky-blue eyes and said in her thick Hungarian accent, "No, darling, I don't understand. Nurses are women."

Although I did not share my grandmother's archaic views on gender roles, the idea of becoming a nurse who cared for children rather than adults was never my intention. I was not a parent then, and I did not know much about kids. Nevertheless, I longed to care for and nurture someone other than myself. In the back of my mind, I knew (hoped) that one day children would play a big role in my life, so I was unconsciously preparing for it. I played my ukulele often and wrote songs that would appeal to a younger demographic including one song called "The Pee Pee Dance"—about the awkward pelvic wiggle that kids perform when they have to, well, pee. Of course, there was a song about poop, too.

I was accepted into nursing school with the plan to care for adult patients. That plan changed when I met my first pediatric patient—the first truly sick child I had ever encountered. I'd never before seen a person in such distress. The girl couldn't have been older than two years old, and she was alone. She was standing up, gripping the rails of the hospital crib, and wailing at the top of her lungs. She was naked except for a pee-engorged diaper which I should have changed, but I was too overwhelmed to know to do so. I was too distracted by the painful-looking red blisters that seemed to cover her entire body. The nurse who was mentoring me that day told me the open lesions were caused by an autoimmune disorder called Steven-Johnson syndrome. When she noticed my horrified expression, she also let me know that the disorder was curable and that this little girl would most likely recover. At that moment, my heart rejoined my body, and I remembered to take a breath.

My job, this nurse informed me right before she raced out of the room to attend to another screaming child, was to stay with this girl and try to calm her. As a mere nursing student, I was not qualified to do much. I definitely did not think I had the ability to help this girl. The simple act of being fully present with this scared human being was a challenge for which I had little preparation. Alone in the room with this crying, hysterical child, I began to feel a bit hysterical myself. Despite my apprehension, I instinctively took her up in my arms and began softly singing a song I had been writing in my head for a while. It began:

NURSE PAPA

I put one foot in front of the other,
I need one hand to cover my eyes.
Like a child who just lost his mother,
too scared even to cry.
But, why must I cry?
I'm too old to drown in tears.
Why must I cry when you're so near?
You are near.

After a few moments, she stopped screaming. Snot dripped down asymmetrically from each of her nostrils. Without even hesitating, I wiped her boogers away with the back of my gloved hand. Tears still clung to her scabby little cheeks and her long black eyelashes. She looked at me silently with giant bloodshot eyes. They were small islands of hazel in two sad pink ponds.

Then, she grabbed my gloved thumb—it filled her entire palm—and pulled it to her face. We just stood there together, she in my arms as I rocked back and forth. When I stopped singing, she started crying, so I started again and continued until she fell silent against me. The room was quiet except for the sound of my song that I had transitioned into a soft humming melody, accompanied by the gentle sway of my body. The girl's head rested heavily upon my shoulder. She was asleep and I could feel her slow breaths on my neck, her beating heart next to mine.

I'd assumed that this little girl had been screaming because of the discomfort from her sores, but I realized that she had simply been scared. She just needed someone to hold her, even if that person was scared as well. As I hugged this child who was a stranger to me, a new awareness began to awake in my brain, but I could not yet name it.

Later that night, as I lay in my own bed, my usual quick and easy slumber alluded me. My mind was still swaying back and forth in that hospital room with that little girl. The song I had been singing to her played on repeat in my head. As I stared at the blank ceiling above me, I realized that never before had I felt so needed by another person. I had never before been able to have such a tangible and immediate impact on someone.

In that moment, it was obvious to me that caring for kids was something I would love doing. I might actually be good at it. I had always related easily to children; they understood and appreciated my odd sense of humor. I was never above performing slapstick or using a ridiculous pun if it would draw out a smile or a laugh. Perhaps all the funny songs I had written and all the silly pictures I had drawn without anybody to share them with would find an audience that would cherish them. The notion that I should begin my career of nursing to children rather than to adults felt like the perfect answer to a question I had never before thought to ask myself. Exhausted, I closed my eyes and fell into a dreamless sleep.

The next week, I told my nursing school adviser that I would be changing my focus of study. I wanted—needed—to be a pediatric nurse. Like most of the big decisions I have made in my life, this one was born out of a hope and with a casual ignorance to many factors beyond my intellectual grasp and control.

Despite my determination, I was blissfully unaware of how incredibly challenging the road I had chosen would be, and how much those challenges would change me. I thought that I learned how to be a nurse while in nursing school, but it turns out that I had merely learned how to be a nursing student.

I eventually discovered—stumbled across, actually—the incredibly wide chasm that exists between nursing theory and nursing practice, the difference between learning something and actually doing it day in and day out. Taking care of these morbidly ill and fragile children on a busy hospital unit would require more patience, resilience, energy, and bravery than I thought I could possess. Often, I simply did not carry these virtues in sufficient amounts to make it through a day emotionally intact.

Six years later, just when I came to believe (audaciously) that I had pretty much figured it all out, I became a parent myself, and the way in which I viewed my role as a nurse was turned on its head. I had thought that I knew how to relate well to my patients and how to thoughtfully interact with their parents, but I had no true awareness of what a parent-child relationship looked and felt like. I possessed only a superficial understanding of that miracle of life, no sleeping, delirious toddler tantrum, seeing the world all over again through a child's eyes type of relationship. I was oblivious to all the pains, joys, frustrations, and revelations that are routine to raising a child—sick or well. As I became more and more acquainted with the challenges of parenting, my understanding of these children and their parents became deeper too. My profound sympathy for their plights took a hiatus, returning transformed into sincere empathy.

I was a nurse to children, but after I became a parent, I realized that I could become so much more to my patients and to my own children too. I could become a Nurse Papa. What that meant to me (among other loftier intentions) was that I would need to parent and nurse from more than one perspective—from the mind of a child, the love and wisdom of a parent, and then, from some place in between. This intention forced me to remember what it felt like to be a child—to sometimes painfully encounter all over again the angst, joy, confusion, and anger of that journey. I would need to approach the kids I work with and the children I was raising in a way that was sensitive to where they were coming from as well as where they hoped to go. Sometimes that destination was a long life, filled with dreams attained and hard lessons learned. Other times, the road was much shorter and overflowing with more pain, heartache, and salvation than I ever thought was possible to fit in one existence.

The very personal journey of parenthood has altered the way I perceive and interact with my young patients. I now have a feeling of comfort and familiarity that I would never have possessed had I not been a parent myself. As these children live and sometimes die, I have learned to be present with them and their families in a way that feels natural and intentional. These lessons do not travel only one way. The challenge of raising my own children has been shaped by my experience of caring for sick ones. I have seen that parenting is infinitely more difficult and frustrating when your child is sick. I have experienced that it is sometimes no picnic even when they are feeling quite well.

The novel revelations I have discovered both in the hospital and from deep within the foxhole of papahood have emerged from places that I did not ever expect. I have learned about the nature of happiness through the lens of great tragedy. I have gained wisdom by being willing to be wrong. I have also accepted that, despite my every instinct to the contrary, taking a step back and doing nothing can sometimes be the most effective parenting strategy. Even though I may remember how I felt about something in the past, I don't know what it will feel like later today, or if that feeling will morph again in the future. This is a journey that is always changing me, because the journey itself is always changing, too.

LEAVING HOME
MORNING STARTS WITH FAMILY

You have a different understanding when you have your own kids. You look at parents and you understand their fear, their anger, their angst, their depression, their caregiver fatigue. There's this understanding that I may not be in your situation, but I see you and I get it in a way that I didn't get before.

– Kate, pediatric oncology nurse, mother

I have been up for many hours and I blame my children. They began making noises long before my alarm clock did. Unable to ignore their restless cries and random rolling around any longer, I escape our full-to-capacity bed and make my way to the kitchen. It is time to get ready for work anyway.

As I tread lightly down the hall, the old hardwood floor follows my feet, squeaking like an out-of-tune mouse orchestra. My son, who has just recently become proficient in the art of walking, escapes the bed too and waddles behind me crying, "Mama MAMAAAA!" while occasionally bumping against the wall of the dark hallway. I forgive his gender confusion. With his pretty blue eyes and wavy blond hair that we have thus far resisted cutting, strangers often mistake him for a girl.

Having finally caught up with me in the kitchen, he is now hugging my leg tightly while looking up at me with a hopeful grin, drooling. I pick him up and we cuddle for a few minutes. His restless head bumps rhythmically against my chest as he doggedly sucks his thumb—his own personal fugue state. His sweet breath on my face and the gurgling sound of the coffee maker take over time and space for a few serene moments.

My son's full diaper breaks the silent spell. It is droopy, wet, but not yet poopy—he saves that for later in the morning—so I change it before I place him down next to my wife, who is still in bed. Before leaving, I look down at my family. They are the three dearest people on this earth to me—the ones who most expertly push my buttons, the ones who tug most stridently at my heart.

My sleeping wife lies on her side, sandwiched between our two children. She, like my son, has never had her hair cut. It reaches almost to the backs of her knees. The evening prior, I watched her braid it with several quick, expert motions before getting into bed. It is a deft ritual full of whipping movements that I love observing, though I have never told her so. Seeing her hair let down makes me feel breathless with affection for her, and I am sometimes left with the fairytale urge to climb it, hand over hand, to the top of a forbidden castle.

In this moment, her long braid winds up around the top of her pillow and past my sleeping daughter's head like a watchful mama serpent. Sssssleeeeep, I imagine it hissing softly to the child below it. My three-year-old daughter rests soundly to her mama's left. When awake, she is hotheaded, an unstoppable force of nature, a closer of bounce houses. Her specialty is the tragic comedy. She once managed to devour an entire bowl of ice cream while at the same time crying that the treat was not only the wrong color, but also not big enough. When asleep though, she is unexpectedly calm and contained. She rests on top of the comforter, her arms stretched out over her head like a bank robber finally giving herself up to the cops.

My boy, half the age of his sister, is still awake and staring at me with a tired smile. He's lying on his belly, his butt in the air. He has found his thumb once again and burrowed his chunky body beneath the crook of my wife's bent arm. His pale skin contrasts sharply with her dark hazelnut complexion. He grabs her hand and pulls it up to his chubby face, so his thumb won't be lonely. He is absolutely addicted to his mama.

"Goodbye, my loves," I say under my breath before heading out the bedroom door, already regretful that I am leaving them. I take one last long look at the restful trio before slipping down the dark hallway again. I will be away from them for fourteen long hours.

When I arrive at the hospital, the fog of sleepiness lingers as I enter the combination code to the nurse break room incorrectly twice before managing to open the door. Usually, I arrive later than this and the place is already humming with the sounds of nurses chatting, laughing, and bitching among themselves. For now, though, the room is empty, and I sadly have no one to talk to. There are the telltale signs of nurses all throughout the room, however. A shiny platter with a few scattered cake crumbs and a frosting-smeared knife. An empty energy drink can lying mournfully on its side next to a pink, serpentine-like stethoscope. The can clearly has no discernible heartbeat or pulse to speak of. Time of death: 1 a.m. There is a nest of hospital blankets left on one of the couches where an exhausted night nurse, who probably did not consume the energy drink, tried to nap a bit during her 3 a.m. break.

I glance quickly at the assignment sheet tacked to the wall to see which kids I will be taking care of, and then make my way to the lone refrigerator that magically serves the cooling needs of so many nurses. As I squeeze my lunch into this already impossibly full fridge, I am greeted by the putrid, eggy waft of some long-neglected food. From behind someone's two-week-old leftover lasagna I imagine the fridge whispering to me: Pssst...pssst. Yeah, you...Empty me out...clean me...please! Although the interior of the fridge is a mess, the outside is bare except for a few flyers and some photographs of past patients. I stop for a moment to look at the picture of an adorable boy who is no longer alive. His name was Rylan.

There have been many photographs of kids displayed on this fridge and all around this room, but most fall away or are eventually removed. So many children pass through our lives—often on the way out of theirs—that it would not make sense for all their photographs to be perpetually displayed. This photograph, though, remains like some mythical, immovable object. I stare at Rylan's sweet face for a moment. He is wearing an oversized chef's hat over his bald head and mixing a bowl of cookie dough. He is not looking at the mixing bowl, nor is he regarding the photographer. Instead, his glance is directed wistfully and a bit impishly toward his dad who sits outside the frame. His dad was never far from him. He still isn't.

I knew Rylan well. When I could make him laugh, it was like striking gold in an iron mine. He once told me he loved me, and tears of joy had welled up in my eyes. Three years ago, and about six months before he died, Rylan handed me a cookie from a batch he had made. With his IV pole trailing behind him like a reluctant robot sidekick on a leash, he excitedly projected in a gravelly voice I can still hear in my head, "Merry Christmas, David! I made cookies for ALL MY NURSES!"

I am snapped back to reality as the room begins to fill up with nurses arriving for the morning shift. Felix, the charge nurse from the night shift, enters the break room. With his manicured goatee, cleanly shaven head, and mischievous smile that never seems to leave his face, he has the air of a swashbuckling pirate. In his requisite blue scrubs and grey beanie that he always wears slightly askew, Felix never looks tired to me. Even after three twelve-hour night shifts in a row, his face looks impeccably fresh. If nurses were birds, he'd be an owl—the one who operates mostly at night even when he is not on the clock. The conversation around the room fades as Felix addresses the nurses in the room.

"Good morning, everybody. Today is Tuesday. The assignments are pretty tight. There are no open beds in the hospital and many expected admissions. We had three nurses call out sick, so we are at minimum. Skill mix is good though. We have lots of experienced nurses today. Help each other out. Fall risks are beds 1, 13, and 24. The watcher is baby Jones in room 3. She has been flirting with sepsis for half the night, and I would not be surprised if she ends up in the PICU this morning. Also, Seth in room 8 is still DNI/DNR. His breathing is agonal and shallow, but we have finally managed to get his pain under control. It looks like he might pass on this shift. There is a lot of family around, and Jen is taking care of him today. Help Jen out when you can. Have a good day, people."

Unrestrained once again, many nurse voices instantly restart their previously paused conversations as the small blue herd slowly streams out of the break room. Like antelopes who are prey to hungry lions, they are picked off by night nurses from the previous shift, each eager to give their own patient reports of the night so they too can leave, sleep. Even though it feels like I have been working all night already, I join this group of nurses, my chosen pack, into the light-filled corridor of this pediatric hospital, our shoes squeaking in unison on the shiny, freshly waxed floors.

RETURNING HOME
THE SEARCH FOR NURSE PAPA

The gravity of what we see and do is fucking exhausting. I have to take time for myself in order to fill myself up again and be present with my own kids. I have put so much pressure on myself to make every day really good—being present all the time, but that is just not realistic. The thought that runs through my mind sometimes is that I have a six-year-old who has lived longer than many of our patients.

— Kate, pediatric oncology nurse, mother

Thirteen hours later, standing in my bathroom at home, I can't wait the thirty seconds necessary for the hot water to arrive from the showerhead. In a disquieting capitulation to the forces of gravity, I stumble into the stream of tepid water.

In an effort to vanquish the faces of sick children from my mind, I focus elsewhere—down upon the scene at my feet. Looking at the penny tile of our shower floor, I see the signs of my children and an earlier bath hour. My daughter's pink flamingo-themed swimsuit, which she now insists on wearing while bathing, is clumped over the drain, preventing the remaining water from retreating. Next to that, plastic Barbie and her best friend Stacey lie naked and frozen in unnatural, ghastly positions. Their frantic-looking hair is wet and splayed across the shiny floor. Two rubber duckies and a turquoise frog with yellow spots on his back silently observe the doll carnage as streams of water quickly wipe away the evidence. Their surprised, white eyes are forever open. I kick the entire crime scene to the corner without ceremony and a half-inch of cold water begins its descent down the drain.

NURSE PAPA

The water from the showerhead is now quite hot. It sprays down upon me, effectively soaking me from head to toe. From brain to heart. From my lungs to my bones. Even my gallbladder, I imagine, tucked safely below my liver, gets a bit wet too. I stand there with my eyes closed and even though I am upright, I feel paralyzed, unable to move. Leaning heavily against the white-tiled wall, I allow the movement of water to massage the day away. A cocoon of steam coats the glass shower walls around me and, for a moment, allows me to exist silently in a space where nobody needs me. The sanctuary is temporary. I can hear the muffled screams of my two kids—it is not clear if they are happy or sad cries—far down the hallway in another part of our home.

I still feel the full weight of the day at work. The children there were sicker and needier than usual, their call lights sending constant and impatient buzzes to the phone tucked into the pocket of my scrubs. I often left a particular room only to be called back a few minutes later to address a beeping machine or assess a new pain and, while I was there, be called to yet another patient. Even as a seasoned nurse, I was overwhelmed by the many complicated and evolving tasks before me, and it was only eight in the morning.

Twelve hours later, exhausted and mentally depleted, I handed off my patients to a fresh-faced night nurse. I changed out of my scrubs and headed for home, armed only with the relief that I would not be returning to the hospital for at least a couple of days. Usually, my commute home is my opportunity to decompress, breathe, listen to a podcast, and maybe even ponder things other than what happened at work. As I biked through the city streets, transferred to a crowded train, and eventually hopped on to my bike again for the last miles home, my mind never left the hospital.

Above the murmuring conversations of fellow commuters

and the banshee screech of the train, I could still hear the screams of a little girl whom I had taken care of that day. She was the same age as my daughter. I had to restrain and poke her multiple times for important blood labs. As she wriggled and screamed on the large hospital bed, her voluminous puff of hair swayed violently like an oversized pom-pom, obscuring her tearful, red face. The rest of her body, held down by me and another nurse, was shockingly still in contrast. Her mom was sitting behind with her arms wrapped around her daughter and, like some tragic Greek statue, crying without tears. These two had already been in the hospital for over a month, and there was no indication that they would be leaving any time soon.

I also could not erase from my mind the sleeping face of a dying teenage girl I visited on my way out. I wondered if she would be alive when I returned. That morning, hurrying between patient rooms dispensing medications and listening to the hearts and lungs of children, I had passed the girl's grandmother in the hall. "Come by. Visit us. Play another happy song for my granddaughter," she requested.

"Of course I will," I said, not knowing when I would make the time. Before I left that evening, and even though she mostly slept through it, I played a lighthearted song of mine on a barely tuned ukulele I had found in her room. The song was about a silly, croaking frog. It began like this:

> *Even if the fish in the sea don't breathe,*
> *don't mean that they don't see you falling.*
> *They're calling.*
> *Even if you're a frog on a lily,*
> *don't mean that you can't be silly,*
> *You're a frog.*

You're croaking.
I never see what it's like to be me.
I walk the street, but these ain't my feet.
How can it be? I still ain't free...

To me, the song is about being yourself and following your instincts—something I sometimes struggle with—and a confusion that parenthood has exacerbated. I had played it often for my own daughter to help her sleep when she was a colicky baby, even though the humorous element of existential angst was lost on her.

That night, as I sat by the teenager's bed, the humor of the song was lost on her as well. Her breaths were deep and calm as she slept. Her hair had been buzzed tightly to her scalp to prevent the indignity of watching it all fall off in irregular clumps, which was yet another form of torture for someone who once had beautiful blonde locks. As I left the room, her father, who had been sitting in the dimly lit corner, looked up at me and nodded, but said nothing.

I arrived home out of breath and eager to relax, but even before I pushed open the front door, I could hear the mayhem within.

"No, Mama! Read it in ENGLISH!" my daughter demanded. When I entered the house, I saw that my beautiful wife was embracing our two squirmy and tearful children on the floor. She was awkwardly holding a bottle of warm milk for our thirsty son while translating a gripping Peppa Pig story written in Spanish back into English for our discerning bilingual daughter.

Having worked her own full day listening to and helping people with their own dire problems, my wife was clearly exhausted. When we locked eyes, she flashed me a silent, Please, save me from these children! plea. Despite the urgency of her expression, the entreaty barely registered in my brain.

Bathed in sweat from the ride home that ended with a steep hill, I forgot to kiss the woman whom I had married just four years earlier. It was a sin that I had been guilty of before and had promised not to repeat.

"I just need a little more sweetness from you at the end of the day," she has often requested of me.

Instead of sweetness though, I grunted flatly, "Hello. How are you?" even though the answer was clear. Without waiting for a reply, I turned my tired body toward the bathroom, leaving a scattered trail of scrubs, socks, and underwear in my wake. I was naked before I got here.

I desperately want to check out, but I can't hide out in the warm water of the shower forever. I can hear my wife attempting to herd our kids to bed and it does not sound like it is going well. I dry off, put on some sweats, and enter the chaos of our living room.

There are toys everywhere. Some are beeping and playing songs, others are lying quiet—innocent victims of AA batteries drained of life. Two massive hills of laundry are piled up on the faux distressed rug, waiting to be folded and put away.

My son, who should be asleep by now, immediately bolts in my direction. He is waving a swollen thumb that, over the first eighteen months of his life, he has precision molded to the upper regions of his palate to sucking perfection. The shaggy mane covering half his face reminds me that a haircut is still in order.

He attaches himself to me, grabbing at my limply hanging arm in a way that normally would feel warm and reassuring, but at this moment feels strangely overbearing. I don't want to be touched, not even by my favorite guy. It is a strange and alien sensation to experience—feeling repulsed by the world and by myself at the same time.

My feisty three-year-old daughter is, like the rug, also faux distressed. She is inexplicably nude from the waist down and jumping on the couch like it is a bounce house. Of course, she chooses this exact moment to make daring demands. After a desultory "Hi, Papa," she yelps in a high-pitched bark, "Dulces! Pink lollipop! I want it! I waaaant it!" She then collapses in feigned syncope onto the couch.

Behind her, my wife shakes her fists and implores toward the ceiling. It is an earnest, but also sarcastic, plea to any of the gods in charge of hyper children. Are they listening?

It is immediately clear that I have entered a not-so-delicate negotiation already in progress, and that I have just unwittingly tapped in. Under normal circumstances, I entertain, if not wholly surrender, to my little girl's ambitious requests. Pint-sized with a high-pitched Minnie Mouse voice to match, she is an exceedingly charming human being. She is beautiful, intelligent, and highly opinionated—just like her mama. When she is not whining, the creative dialectic she uses to achieve her various toddler desires is highly entertaining and, at times, inspiring. I do not know a person in this world who takes more joy in small pleasures than my daughter. She can nurse a lollipop for days. She makes an enthusiastic and ape-like hooting noise in anticipation of any prize won. It usually feels good to be part of that celebration.

This night is different though. People who actually needed things, I think to myself, had been asking me for them all day and had usually done so much more politely. Now, at the end of the day, I have nothing left to give. My daughter, appropriately oblivious, continues with her pleading that quickly devolves into a long and protracted whine, and then to an all-out body-writhing, floor-pounding tantrum.

"Stop yelling...stop it...STOP YELLING!" I yell, fully aware of the hypocrisy of my frantic demand. I grab at my forehead with both hands and unleash a long, animal-like groan from deep within my throat. My half-naked daughter immediately stops her contrived screaming, for a moment becomes mute, and then begins hysterically crying.

"Mama, Mama! Papa yelled at me," she sobs in the direction of the kitchen where my wife has retreated with our son. However, I can barely hear her as I have already, like a tantrum-y toddler myself, stormed out of the room. But, unlike the age-appropriate emotional breakdown of a little girl, mine was angry, even a bit wild. Without even brushing my teeth or flossing—nighttime rituals that I almost never skip—I collapse onto our bed and bury myself under the covers. My wet hair leaves a large damp spot on the pillow below me, but I do not care. I fall asleep almost instantly.

The next morning, I wake up feeling more rested. I had slept close to ten hours, a feat that is almost unheard of these days. My uninterrupted rest certainly meant that my equally tired wife had been up multiple times during the night to care for one child and then another. As I stretch my arms up and peel my eyes open, I relive my behavior from the night before as if it were part of a dream—a nightmare, really. I feel guilty for losing my temper, even though in that moment, any form of restraint had felt impossible. Despite my regret and my rest, a heavy residual malaise from the previous day hangs on my body like an extra layer of skin. I am not ready to get up yet.

Glancing around the room, I notice a small pile of parenting books on the nightstand, all of which I have failed to read because I simply did not want to, though I knew I should want to. The three well-regarded titles that focus on different aspects of child-rearing are partially concealed by a larger pile of New Yorker magazines that I definitely do want to read, but also have not. A fine coat of dust, marred only by the smudged, yogurt-y handprint of one of my children, covers the top magazine. Upon that lies my yellowing mouthguard that I failed to put in the night before. It smiles sadly at me. I frown back.

Before my daughter was born, I would sometimes attempt to read one of those parenting books before falling asleep. It focused on childbirth and the first year of a child's life. Important stuff, of course, but no matter how many times I tried, I never managed to get past the sentence So, you're having a baby...before falling into a deep and untrammeled sleep. Those books were better than melatonin, but they did not teach me a thing about being a dad.

Still lying in bed and not ready to move, I recall an incident a year prior when I had lost my temper in a manner like the previous evening. I had been helping my daughter out of her crib when, with no obvious motive, she slapped me hard across the face. This was no accident, and when the first blow was not satisfying enough for her, she went for another swipe. With this second attempt, she only injured the air in front of my face. In any case, the damage, all of it emotional, had already been done. My daughter sits happily at 6% on the growth chart and at that time was no more than twenty-three pounds soaking wet, but when she dared to hit me, her papa, I nearly lost it.

In my anger and frustration, I picked her up and screamed way too loudly, "YOU DO NOT HIT PEOPLE! YOU DO NOT HIT YOUR PAPA!" and stormed away in a huff. From the kitchen, I could hear my wife consoling our hysterical daughter and picking up the emotional pieces that I had left strewn about.

I heard my daughter asking her mama, "Where Papa? Where

Papa?" She had, during that time, taken to asking this question whenever I became visibly flustered or upset, sometimes as I stood right beside her.

In moments of self-pity, I ask myself the very same question my daughter posed to my wife that day: Where Papa? Because, very often, nurse me and papa me feel like two very different people. At work, when a sick child has an epic tantrum, or lashes out at me or their parents, I am almost always able to maintain a cool and calm reserve. I am the even-tempered presence in the room who is able to give advice that I surely would never be able to follow if it were me with my own child. I am able to step back from the pain and chaos that my patients experience in a way that is unimaginable with my own two children. When my own kids are suffering or are making me suffer, it assaults me on a genetic level. I feel it in every cell in my body. I can't escape it even when I most desire to do so. It is painful to admit that, at times, I am the man I have always strived to be with my young patients and their parents, while being at my worst with my kids and my wife.

I don't know if I will ever consistently be the best version of myself or if that aspiration is even possible for me. During hard times especially, I wonder about the qualities of Nurse Papa, the superhero parent and caregiver that I evoke in my hopeful imaginings. His superpower is the ability to be the best dad and the best nurse all the time. He always knows the right words to say. He never loses his temper. He never runs away when life gets hard.

Occasionally, I am able to step out of my role as a self-diagnosed dysfunctional dad and actually summon Nurse Papa at home, to be him for a short while with my own kids too. I envy myself in those moments, just as I predict the times in the future when I will surely fall short of my best intentions. I wonder if I ever will be the best dad I can be, at least part of the time. Will it take me ten years raising my two kids to feel like a competent parent on a daily basis? Will they survive, emotionally intact, long enough for me to get there?

Many of my nurse colleagues struggle with this too. Corianna is a nurse whom I admire to a fault. I marvel at her ability to recognize the pain in others and her skill to fix that pain. She also possesses the confidence and wit to say the most inappropriate things at the most appropriate moments. Corianna shared with me that she too struggles with the same tension that I do.

"Nursing is my life," she told me one day. "But I still haven't figured out how to create a successful life outside of work. My husband will say to me, 'I want the you that you are at work. I want it at home'...At work I am a different person. [Nursing] feeds me emotionally and socially. Taking care of people is my life, but I don't know why I can't take care of my family like that."

When she told me that, we were sitting together in her home on a plush grey couch covered generously with white dog hair. The origin of the hair was sitting a foot away, growling menacingly at me as if I were an intruder intending to hurt his mom. Corianna's daughter was watching a movie in another room. She occasionally yelled across the house to her mom to come help her with something she was very capable of doing herself.

With an exaggerated eye roll that only I could see, though her daughter certainly must have sensed it through the wall, Corianna yelled back, "You can do it yourself. Don't make me come over there," before sighing cartoonishly and going to her. Despite Corianna's believable claim that she and her cute daughter were codependent best friends, I could feel in that moment how challenging motherhood and life at home must sometimes feel to her. Regardless of the many joys that come with spending time with my own kids, I often feel the same way.

A few days after my outburst in the living room, my daughter and I find ourselves facing off once again. It is late—far past her bedtime—yet she refuses to lie down no matter how many times I beg her to do so. Having not gone to work today, I am less tired and perhaps more patient than I would have been after a long, hard day at the hospital. Deciding to let her parent herself for once, I leave the room to give her the space to figure it out on her own.

Eventually, she falls asleep with her arms and legs splayed akimbo among the pile of toys with which she had been communing on the floor. She snores in unison with the familiar melody of "Wheels on the Bus," which still plays softly from the phone I had left for her earlier. I stand and watch her. It is the best scene I have witnessed in quite a while. My wife has often stated that our daughter appears the most beautiful and peaceful when she is asleep, and I tend to agree with her. The girl never screams, "No Papa!" when she is sleeping.

For a moment, standing in the doorway of my daughter's room, I am transported back to a time when she was just a baby. Back then, she did not fight me like she does now. Her eccentric personality, so packed full of willfulness and quirky fears, had not yet dared to crawl out of its tiny pink baby cave. During that time, I actually believed that this sweet, sweet child could and would never do wrong. I remember naively expressing this feeling to some of my nurse coworkers who had older kids. They smiled knowingly back at me, well aware of the travesty of toddlerhood that lay shortly ahead for me.

After a while of watching my daughter sleep, I begin to feel tired myself. A long Wookie yawn arches its way through my entire body.

This feeling of weariness is soon replaced by a feeling of longing. I miss my wife. With all the chaos of the last few days, we have not found time to connect or talk about anything beyond the mechanics of parenting. More often than not, raised voices from different ends of the house represent our main source of communication as we each tend to a separate child.

My wife is in the living room now, engaged in one of her favorite late-night activities—nibbling on a piece of dark chocolate while watching a cooking show on television. I want to cuddle with her on our too-small couch. I need to feel close to her again, to remember why we love each other and why we were so excited to bring kids into this world to be a part of that love.

Before I join my wife, I pick up my daughter's tiny limp body from the floor of her room and place her gently down in her bed. I whisper "Good night, my love" in her ear and kiss her spotless forehead. She does not wake up.

DAVID METZGER, R.N.

BREAK FROM THE HEARTBREAK
A Slice of Fatherhood

You're pregnant? Again?

– Nurse Papa

As I stared blankly at the sad slice of pizza smashed upon the cement floor of a crowded Costco, I gently pondered the phenomena of hitting parental rock bottom. More specifically, I wondered if I might have just done that. My newborn son was snoring soundly against my chest. He was oblivious to the curious stares of weekend shoppers that penetrated the back of my neck all the way to my delicate psyche. Although I was keenly aware that I was the center act of Costco in that moment, I felt no embarrassment, only a detached numbness. How did I get here? I wondered. Where was here, anyway?

Before I was a father, I foolishly considered myself to be somewhat of an expert in the hearts and minds of children, and one uniquely equipped to maintain my cool when those hearts and minds erupted. I had taken care of thousands of kids. I had seen close up what makes many of them tick and, often, how to work around those things. I learned very quickly, though, that being a parent is infinitely more difficult and complicated than caring for the children of others.

If I had considered the realities of fatherhood before I attained that status, I probably assumed that it would be fun most of the time and that I would be pretty good at it. While this is often the case, the reality of making it through the day with my kids usually takes precedence over all the fun I once anticipated. That is where the joke of parenting really began for me: in the vast difference between my expectations of parenthood and the controlled chaos and emotional turbulence that it actually is. I often find myself yelling at my two kids even though I don't always remember what I was upset about in the first place. Yelling at my children might be something I partake in too often, second only to chasing after them with a cordless dust buster aimed in their general direction.

When we had only one child, I had no inkling about how the addition of another would lead to an exponential factor of pleasure and pain. I wish I could say that more experienced parents than myself had failed to warn me just how difficult it would be, but they had. Many times. All of those whom I had asked (and many I had not) warned me all about it. I simply failed to believe them. If I did believe them in my heart, the notion somehow lost its way on the curvy path to my smug brain.

Thirty-six hours into my second child's pink, pudgy life, he came online and spent most of the night screaming. Loudly. In his short and sleepy existence, this seemed to be the first moment in which he grasped that he was no longer tucked warmly away in the womb of his mommy, and he was pissed about it. I tried to cradle him while gently bouncing up and down on a large exercise ball. This method had worked well when his older sister was a crying infant. It also did wonders for my dad bod. Now though, the bouncing only seemed to upset this strange new life form. Do baby tricks expire? I thought dimly to myself as I continued bouncing mindlessly. My son's cries woke up his older sister, who soon added her own screams to our miserable baby chorus. Their two-person show went on all night.

The next day, my wife and I were both worn out. Left adrift

in a murky parental storm, we deduced that only a misdirected and poorly executed plan—a weekend trip to Costco with the new baby and my mother-in-law in tow—would help. Fools we were.

We arrived at the giant parking lot and, after a brief argument about the merits of remaining patient for a space close to the front, we found a compact space into which we barely squeezed our mid-size SUV. Upon entering the vast commercial cavern that is Costco, my senses were immediately and overwhelmingly assailed by the many sights, sounds, and smells big-boxing my brain.

Somehow, we made our way around the flat-screen televisions, phones, and other shiny gadgets that all seemed to be talking to each other in different beeping and chirping languages. We pushed on, even though the rickety shopping cart I had chosen only wanted to turn an awkward left.

Unfortunately, we had only just begun to enter the real jungle— the food aisles. In every direction, massive shelves of packaged food towered to the ceilings. In their shadows, tiny Filipina women wearing starched red aprons offered us a myriad of fake food samples: gluten-free meatballs, dehydrated pineapples slices, and salmon jerky.

As I contemplated why some jerk had decided it was a good idea to jerk salmon, I was quickly losing the composure I had gathered after the previous night's noise rodeo. Through the mental fog, I deduced that I needed immediate nourishment if I were to continue with this perilous journey of material consumption. It was well past noon. We had not eaten breakfast nor sipped a drop of coffee before leaving the house. My stomach growled like an empty garbage truck at the beginning of its route. It was a tactical error that I vowed not to repeat. I separated from the family pack and, with my son snoring against my chest, headed for the Costco cafeteria.

The line for food was ten consumers deep, which allowed me just enough time to decide which processed food item to order. I don't know why I decided that a greasy, 700-calorie combo slice of pizza would be the best meal to start the day. The glistening mushrooms, peppers, and sausage bits knew I was weak. They sizzled together in a bed of melted cheese and called my name seductively.

I clumsily poised the piece above my mouth just like a statue of Bacchus would have, had he been interested in pizza rather than grapes. A translucent line of yellowish grease dripped down my wrist. In my haste to shove the entire slice of pizza into my mouth while not dripping hot cheese on the head of my sleeping newborn son, I fumbled and dropped the slice onto the dirty cement floor. It met the ground cheese-side down with a disquieting plop. A clump of tomato sauce came to rest on my shoe, silently jeering at me. What followed was an adult tantrum that would be the envy of most aspiring Shakespearean actors. Did Hamlet enjoy bulk shopping?

I am not proud of what occurred next. I did not simply drop the pizza on the floor, clean it up like any normal adult should, purchase an equally greasy and bloat-provoking hotdog, and then move on with my life. No. After a moment of disbelief, I fell to my knees, picked up the slice, stared at it in anger, and then slammed it down on the floor in what can best be described as a childish rage. I knelt over that triangular mess before me, for a moment giving the pizza an opportunity to explain itself. It did not. It would not. It simply could not.

A curious ring of shoppers circled around me, watching. To their credit, there was not an unsympathetic face in the bunch, but despite their good intentions, they were clearly waiting to see if this sad man with a newborn smashed to his chest, and his pizza smashed to the ground, would do anything else ridiculous. This was definitely the most exciting thing going on at Costco—far better than the free salmon jerky samples for sure. The bystanders must have been asking themselves, Will he eat the pizza now? Will he smash it on the floor again? Does he need a hug? Should someone call security? Does Costco even have security?

That day in Costco, I acted just like a two-year-old when he simply does not get what he wants—just like my daughter, actually. Her worst public explosion began at the start of a six-hour flight when she was only a three-year-old. She was just old enough to have her own seat, but young enough to not want anything to do with it. As soon as we left the ground, she refused to be restrained by her seat belt even in its loosest possible orientation. She then escaped from the confinement of her outfit and ripped off her diaper with a harrowing Klingon yell. Every attempt to cover or calm her was met with resistance.

After close to an hour of jumping, screaming, wriggling, and growling in her birthday suit (she thinks every day is her birthday), she eventually tired herself out and retreated under the seat in front of her. I'm pretty sure the airline attendants were aware of her gross noncompliance with TSA safety rules, but they knew better than to intercede. Don't wake the beast, please, I pleaded with my tired papa eyes, and they thankfully ignored the girl who was sleeping under the seat, a Jet Blue blanket wrapped around her tiny body.

It has taken me a while to accept the supremely sucky moments of early parenthood as equal in worth to the absolutely amazing times I routinely experience with my kids—the quotidian joy they bring me. Each experience is important. Those hard moments, when I am pulling the hair from my head in frustration, and those glorious times, when I am bursting with so much love I feel like

I might just explode, seem to come from the same place. Within this magical world live all the hopes, dreams, and unreasonable expectations that I hold for my kids as people and for myself as a parent. It is during these times that I feel most perfectly imperfect and so humbly human; when I am both evolving and regressing at the same time.

One of the reasons I felt driven to have kids is that I was weary of always being the center of my own universe. I wanted to focus on something other than my own needs and myopic insecurities. What I did not expect to learn is that the experience of raising children actually sharpens my focus on who I am and who I wish to be. It places my flaws under a microscope and allows me to view them in an entirely new close-up way. The novel experience of parenthood has escalated my emotional growth process. My kids have become my unwitting teachers, and they don't hand out hall passes—even when I really need to pee.

On the very next flight we took, my daughter behaved admirably and we were far better equipped (iPad and snacks). She still did request to remove all her clothes mid-flight, but it was a polite petition and she gracefully relented when we asked her to refrain. I don't know what about being at 30,000 feet in the air prompts my daughter's nudist desires, but it was notable that she listened to us this time without much fuss.

There was another child on that same flight who was not faring as well. He was a few years older than our girl and he was screaming incessantly and at an excruciatingly loud volume for the entire last half of the flight. It sounded to me like some unseen surgeon must be slowly removing one of the boy's kidneys sans anesthesia. I felt for him and his family. His stressed-out mom was on her own and responsible for another very young child as well. That poor mom, I thought, as our own two kids slept soundly across both our laps. She will be a wreck by the time we land. Contrary to my expectations, when I got a better look at the mom as she exited the plane with her two exhausted children, she appeared mostly calm and relaxed (Xanax, perhaps?). Clearly, she had been through epic organ-removing breakdowns, such as the one we had just witnessed, many times prior. She must have developed a calm equanimity that allowed her to come out clean on the other side knowing, indeed, that things can always get much worse. She must have learned as well that no matter how difficult life may seem, the storm is always darkest right before the clear skies return.

BE A PARENT FOR TODAY

We knew it was a really bad diagnosis from the onset. I would tell Ari, "Don't go on the internet because the statistics are really bad and old. We just need you to be that one person. If you are that one, then the statistics don't matter and we will do everything we can do for you."

- Susan, Ari's mom

For me, becoming a parent was like stepping into the abyss. Even though literally billions of humans had walked the same path, some leaving behind tales of their journeys, I still did not know what to expect. Even today, six years in, the experience of raising my kids feels novel. It is a daily experiment in trying to be a good person and guiding my children to be the same.

Before my wife and I brought our two goofy kids into this world, neither of us had spent much time contemplating if it would be a world worthy of them being born into. We just wanted kids. We wanted a family together and did not question that urge. Aside from our mutual attraction and a penchant for making each other laugh, our strong desire to be parents was a big part of why we thought we would be good for each other. It was not until our children arrived that I began to consider the implications of what we had done. I sometimes lie in my bed late at night, pondering the ceiling and all the doom-filled uncertainties of the world my kids will one day be adults in. Climate change, the current pandemic we are all living through, and so many other chilling prospects that seem to have especially plagued the last year, make me wish that I had contemplated my decision to be a papa more thoughtfully.

The routine threat to the happiness and longevity of the people I hold most dear sometimes leaves me feeling helpless. It is an emotional burden that I neither conceived of nor planned for when my children were just a happy fantasy for the future. It is a challenge for me to be the best dad today when I don't know what the future holds for tomorrow.

The parents I meet in the hospital must consider a future drastically different from what they once anticipated for their child. Until cancer interrupted their lives, these moms and dads probably never considered the possibility that their teenage son might not be well enough to one day attend high school, or that their little girl might not live long enough to perform in her first dance recital. These parents must discover for themselves the best way to raise their child when each new day is the only thing they can possibly look forward to. Their emotional and intellectual journeys have shown me ways in which I, too, might navigate an uncertain future for my kids.

In my time as a nurse, I have sat with countless parents as they learn of their child's diagnosis. I have also seen how this diagnosis shaped their relationship with their child throughout their illness. Most parents will never forget how they felt when they learned that their child has cancer, how that news changed them. This moment is often the beginning of their reorientation as parents of a sick child.

Before we begin any real treatment, the parents and their doctors sit down in a room and participate in what is called a consent conference. During the consent conference, our doctors undergo the often Herculean effort of educating parents about the treatment options for their child, as well as the possible side effects of these therapies. The amount of information can be dizzying. Parents must take in all this information while navigating through a vast array of emotions. I have witnessed parents cry and wail to their gods as the medical team disseminates the bad news and its implications. Other parents take the news with an eerie stoicism, as if to save their emotional energy for when they will truly need it most. The pediatric patient rarely attends these conferences, in part because of the unpredictability of their family's responses. Kids need to see their parents as a source of strength. These parents often need time to summon that strength.

Nurses often attend these meetings. At one such meeting, a monolingual father needed a Spanish interpreter. I speak enough Spanish to have understood much of what this father asked before the translator related it back to the medical team. So, when this heartbroken and exhausted man cut right to the chase and said to the doctors, "Díganme verdad, hay una cura?" (Tell me the truth. Is there a cure?), I heard his sad words twice and, as a father myself, it was difficult to hold back my tears. The doctors responded honestly but without commitment, because no one can guarantee a specific outcome.

"This is a very difficult disease to cure and your daughter's symptoms are not what we normally observe," one doctor replied. "We'll know a lot more once we see how she responds to treatment."

The father looked back at the doctors, and with tired, bloodshot eyes said, "Dios me dio esta niña porque el sabia que yo cuidaría de ella. Dios no nos da lo que no podemos manejar... Haz lo que tengas que hacer. Confío en todos ustedes" (God gave me this child because he knew I would care for her. God doesn't give us what we can't handle. Do what you must. I trust you.) He slapped the table lightly in what appeared to be an act of resolution and strength.

Then, the walls fell. He lowered his head and began to cry softly. I quickly handed him a box of tissues even as I attempted to hide my own tears. I try not to burden parents with my own emotions when I can prevent it, but I was caught off guard in that moment. I teared up for him and for his daughter—a girl who had already shown herself to be way too sweet for cancer. I knew that this was just the beginning for this family.

During the rest of the meeting, the dad repeated intermittently and almost as a whispered mantra to himself, "I just want my daughter back. I just want her back." It seemed like he was already mourning a lost childhood and a fatherhood very different from what he had once expected. "I have three kids. We are a family of five," he said, as if he were reminding himself of his family unit that was now being pulled apart. His voice was clipped and shaky, not only due to his limitations with English, but because he was overcome by emotion.

In that moment, I noticed the white t-shirt he was wearing. It was stained and had a few holes near the neckline. His arms were covered with fading, amateurish tattoos and his rough hands had specks of what looked like paint on them. This man is a laborer, I thought. He knows about hard work and is not afraid of it.

For this father, though, facing his fear regarding his daughter's uncertain future was an altogether new challenge of faith and hope— one that would force him to ask what kind of parent he needed to be for his daughter on that tragic day, and then all the days after.

Over the months that followed, I encountered him a few more times. Every time we spoke, it was clear that each moment of fatherhood felt like an act of creation for him. To be fluid was the only way he could manage. He was forever attempting to figure out what being a dad to his newly sick daughter meant to him.

Amy, a nurse friend of mine who has taken part in many consent conferences, told me that most parents don't fully absorb all the implications that come with a cancer diagnosis: "They don't know that this may mean that their kids won't be able to have children of their own. There are so many long-term effects of chemotherapy, but when you are in the moment, all you are thinking is 'Save my kid.' You're not thinking about their hearing or their kidney function because you want them to live. You aren't thinking about what this might mean for two years down the road or five years down the road. You're just thinking, 'Save my kid tonight!'"

After the initial shock wears off, many parents discover that they not only have to reorganize their lives to care for their child, but they must also reorient how they feel and act as parents. In our culture, so much about how we raise our kids revolves around preparing them for their future and getting them ready for life. Living with a sick child or caring for a dying one turns that intention upside down. You have to focus on each day.

Susan, whose son Ari was diagnosed with a very aggressive cancer in his early twenties, told me that the near certainty of Ari's poor prognosis helped shape her relationship with her son. It also altered her entire worldview as a parent. "Whenever we were in the hospital, I would think that this might be the absolute best day we ever would have. I just really wanted to be in that day, wherever it was. It was just part of my reality."

What Susan wanted for her son, she explained, was that he would never feel he was alone. She would always say, "We've got chemo," or "We've got radiation tomorrow," in a way that inserted her into his treatment. His emotional, if not physical burden, became hers to bear as well.

Susan and Ari spent a lot of time together both inside and

outside the hospital, allowing them to strengthen an already special bond. They took long walks, played cards, talked about everything, and just generally enjoyed each other's company.

"He called himself a mama's boy," Susan said, "and he didn't care who knew it." They truly became buddies who found comfort in each other, even in the most uncomfortable of situations. Because Susan and Ari's relationship existed so much in the present, it evolved into a profoundly deep connection between them.

"There really wasn't any bullshitting," Susan told me. "This was life and death. It was stripped bare."

I had once assumed that all parents of sick children would need to fully devote their time to finding a cure that could save their child, but the truth is much more nuanced. Two parents, Jason and Krisi, showed me that accepting what you cannot control can also be a gift.

Their son Rylan, the boy whose photograph still graces the side of the break room refrigerator, knew that his parents loved him more than anything in this world. That's all he needed to know. There was rarely a time when they were not both by his side during his many long stays in the hospital. In each room they occupied, Jason marked out a mini basketball court with masking tape so Rylan could practice his shooting, so he could be a kid. He and Krisi watched their son with joy and restrained trepidation as he tossed endless layups and jump shots up to the small basket attached to the wall, his IV pole playing the role of a hapless defender. Rylan preferred to shoot hoops along with the beats and rhythms of the latest Justin Timberlake jam oozing in the background.

Don't be so quick to walk away, dance with me...

Rylan hits a beautiful shot from the outside.

...I wanna rock your body, please stay, dance with me...

A nothing-but-net jump shot.

...You don't have to admit you wanna play, dance with me...

Another arching shot from the outside.

Rylan did not even look up to see the orange foam ball bounce off the rim and drop soundlessly to the floor. He danced in his joy for life, not in celebration of a shot made. It was a joy his parents helped foster. In a very real way, the possibility of Rylan's premature death helped Jason and Krisi to give Rylan what he truly needed—a life worth living and fighting for.

After Rylan died, Jason told me that he and Krisi never treated their son like a sick kid. Even though they wanted to protect him, they were more afraid of him losing his spirit or missing out on the rare gift of childhood. When Rylan wanted to shoot hoops, they let him do it even though they were nervous that he might hurt himself. Although Jason and Krisi may have felt powerless to cure their son, they did have the power to help him live the way he wanted to. Rylan knew how he wanted to live his life. He wanted to play basketball. He wanted to dance.

Rylan's parents, like so many others I have encountered in the hospital, have gifted me a useful point of view. It is a mindset of humble gratitude for all the daily joys my children experience, and a hopeful optimism for the ones they might one day luckily encounter. I've learned to cherish every moment with my kids, even the hard ones in which parenthood feels like a job I should have avoided. If it all ends tomorrow or ten years from now, I can now accept that all these moments—good and bad—will have been enough for me to justify becoming a parent to two wonderful kids in this uncertain world.

Even a life that is fleeting can be a life well lived. When I first meet a child like Rylan who has a rough diagnosis, I sometimes cannot help but put them into a category of kids who will die young. To do otherwise would run counter to the painful realities I witness every day. To accept that these kids will die does not mean that I don't have hope for them, though. Rather, I hope that each day these children live, they do so in a way that makes them feel happy and fulfilled. I hope that they have things to look forward to, that they smile often. I also hope that they are able to express their feelings—the good and the bad—to those they love. If they are able to do these things, then it is a gift. It is a gift for today and tomorrow.

FAMILY IS WHERE YOU FIND IT

The hospital gave them family.

- Amy, pediatric oncology nurse, mother

Kids don't need to be taught to love. This drive comes as natural to their hearts as breathing does to their lungs. It is from their parents and others who care for them that children learn how to express this love. We show by example. When my daughter is scared or sad, I do not possess the magic formula that will make it all better. In those times, the only thing I can do is get down on my knees—right at her level—and hug her. This simplest of gestures is my way of showing her that I care, of saying, I'm here for you and I'm not going anywhere. I can't, I'm on my knees.

In the hospital, I also spend a great deal of time kneeling next to my patients so that they too know I care. I remember clearly when I first consciously experienced the intimate power of meeting a person eye to eye. I was a very small boy. It was a Saturday morning and my dad was kneeling before me. He was wearing beige pin-striped pajamas, and he still had a prominent bedhead from the night before. There was sleep in his eyes, but there was something else there too—a few stray tears. In a slow, steady voice he told me that his father—my grandfather—had died. In that moment, my dad was looking right into my eyes with both his hands resting gently on my shoulders. I remember how his slender fingers fell so softly on my skin, how each digit sported a small tuft of curly black hair. Then, he pulled me in for a long, warm hug. What I took away from that moment, so many years ago, is not the sadness and inevitability of death, but rather the feeling of safety and closeness I felt from my father. It was the feeling of family.

I have learned, though, that you do not need to be related to be a family. The people drawn to this hospital by occupation and by illness often band together to create a similar bond usually found among blood relatives. They are brothers and sisters who share the experience of being young and sick. They are mothers and fathers joined in their heartache and their hope.

For many of these parents, it is important that we nurses are deeply affected by the humanity of their children. We are witnesses to their child's journey in a way that nobody else is. When their child dies, they lose us too. It is a double tragedy for them. The support system they once depended upon is no longer there, constantly entering their space, joking with them, caring for their child, and holding their pain. We help carry their emotional burden just as members of a family would.

In this hospital home, we all live and breathe together, along with all the fun and dysfunction that is bound to exist among such a diverse set of people. Sometimes we thrive. Often we struggle, but we rarely do it alone.

One day, I found myself kneeling by the bedside of one of my older patients. His name was Mohammed and he was in his mid-twenties. His cancer had returned, and he was on his own. His family lived overseas, and they were rarely able to be at the hospital with him.

"The doctors say that I probably have less than a year left to live," he told me soon after I entered his room.

"I heard," I responded. I should have felt uneasy discussing this boy's imminent death, but I did not. "That must be an incredibly overwhelming reality to deal with. You don't deserve this, Mo. I'm glad to see you, though. You are looking well and...happy."

Mohammed just sat there in his bed, a sanguine smile on his patchy bearded face and a relaxed manner that in this context would have surprised most people. I had grown accustomed to his even-keeled attitude.

"It's just the way I have always been—even when I was a little kid," he once told me when I asked him about it. "I don't have much time left, I know, and any time I spend feeling sad or depressed is time that I'm just not being myself; time when I am already dead... Hakuna Matata," he said with a wry smirk.

Hakuna Matata. No Worries. What a wonderful way to live. The lyrics from that cheerful Lion King song played in my mind as I knelt next to Mohammed's bed. What an amazing way to die, I thought to myself.

When Mohammed was first diagnosed with his disease, he was so disoriented from the delirium of the hospital and the many drugs clouding his brain that he very nearly lost his mind. He was not himself. Late one night in the hospital, he became confused and yanked out the central line that entered through his arm and traveled all the way to his heart. His blood was everywhere and, as his nurses tried to calm him, he was screaming clearly yet incoherently. As he regarded in disbelief the blood covering his chest and hands, he kept yelling up to the lights above him and the nurses working swiftly around him, "I killed someone! I think I killed someone!"

Ironically, at almost that exact same moment and a few rooms away, a young girl named Lisa died from her disease. But Mohammed had nothing to do with that. Lisa's mother was also not with her. For days after, nurses who were working together with those two patients would recount the eerie confluence of those two moments and the tragedies that bring strangers so close, if not together.

As I knelt beside him, Mohammed was himself again, even though he too was slowly dying. He was not happy about that reality, he assured me, but he was at peace with the inevitability of it. He told me that he had just recently broken the news of his poor prognosis to his brother and mother. It was clear from his telling that he took more care for their feelings than he did for his own. He just wanted them to be okay with the cruel fate he had already calmly resigned himself to. This characteristic selflessness reminded me of a time, months earlier, when Mohammed was first diagnosed. The doctors wanted to use his cancer cells for a research study. He consented to participate because it might help people like him not experience pain, but he would agree to it "only if the mice in the experiments were treated nicely." The mice.

Mohammed and I talked and laughed together as I knelt by his bedside. He told me about his time away from the hospital and the awkward deficits of his disease that he somehow found grace in. Though highly deconditioned and out of shape, he had recently been able to hit some golf balls with his older brother. He seemed so elated to learn that he could still hit the ball even though it was always a weak stroke and in the wrong direction. Soon after Mohammed found out that his tumor had returned—this time all over his body—his close friends had thrown him a huge party, which he knew would probably be his last.

"The whole night I had this huge smile on my face," he said. "It was amazing to see so many people cared about me, even people who barely knew me. I've never had so much fun in my life. It was my death party."

In turn, I told Mohammed about a party we had just thrown

for my son. He had just turned one year old the week before. When Mohammed asked for it, I showed him a picture of my family from that party day. In the photo, we are all wearing funny headbands with antennas—it was a bug-themed party—and squinting in the bright midday sun. We are all holding each other tightly. Mohammed looked at the photo for a long moment, taking in the details of the silly scene.

"I would not be able to contain my joy if I had what you have," he said with no trace of envy. His glassy eyes locked with mine until I had to look away.

In the quiet of his hospital room, without anything to distract us, it felt easy to listen and share with each other these small details of our lives. Here in this place where there is often no cure, there exists something else that we can give and receive. To be present and undistracted, to acknowledge a person's joy or their fears without agenda, is a gift that I have come to expect as normal around here. It's what family does.

Without saying it, I let Mohammed know that I cared about him deeply, that I saw him. With his smile and gracious manner, he revealed to me his beautiful courage and uncommon wisdom. He also showed me that I had a purpose in his life other than to administer chemotherapy. That I could be useful to him even though I was powerless to save him. That I was family.

Every one of us belongs to a family—some that we were born into and others that we have found and become part of. To me, the singular quality of family is that its members know and accept each other for who they are and what they are going through. We are there for each other during the mundane moments to share a smile or a joke. We are there, too, for the life-changing times, in which our presence is our only power. When people let their guard down and bare their innermost feelings and fears, their vulnerability is a powerful act of creation. What they create is a family, and we are all part of it.

BREAK FROM THE HEARTBREAK
BEN BEEPS

We process things through humor in a way that other people would be offended by.

- Ashley, pediatric oncology nurse, mother

When Ben first learned that he had leukemia, he was all alone. He had just started college. He later told his mom, Jaclyn, how afraid he had felt in that strange hospital with no support. He didn't ever want to be left alone again in a hospital, he told her. Jaclyn took that request to heart. She never left Ben alone again, except, of course, when he asked her to go.

Ben probably did not say it explicitly, but on this day, he needed some space. It was the NBA finals and his team, the Warriors, were playing. It was months before we would tell this twenty-year-old boy that he no longer had any viable therapy options. On this day, though, there was still hope. The Warriors were also looking good.

We were still trying to prepare Ben for a possible second bone marrow transplant, and I had just begun administering a high-risk therapy which made it necessary for me to keep a close eye on him. Various wires stuck to his pale chest and led to a monitor overhead. Any time his vital signs deviated from where they were supposed to be, the monitor alerted me with a series of staccato beeps.

That afternoon, Ben and his monitor had been relatively quiet as he attentively watched the game on TV. About halfway through the game, though, the monitor went off, sending an alarm to my phone that Ben had become apneic, meaning that he was no longer breathing. I quickly dashed out of another patient's room and ran to Ben's room. He was perfectly well, leaning forward in bed and intently watching his game. If anything, Ben seemed a bit surprised by my out-of-breath burst into his tranquil basketball space. After a few more incidents like that, I began to wish that I had remembered to put on deodorant that morning.

I soon realized that Ben's "apneic episodes" were caused by his reaction to the game. Every time our famous point guard poised for a three-point shot, Ben held his breath. Just as it swished into the net, Ben's monitor interpreted his bated breath as apneic, setting off all the lights and beeps. When we figured out what was happening, he and I chuckled together. I silenced the beeping monitor and left Ben alone to be with his team. Until the game was over, Ben would be on his own.

SAYING GOODBYE TO YOUR KIDS

*They cleaned him up as much as they could. He had so much blood on him.
They gave us private time with him. We held him and talked to him like he
was still there. It is weird when you look at someone who has just passed. It is
a shell of them. You instantly know that their spirit went somewhere.*

- Jason, Rylan's dad

For some parents, saying goodbye to their children, even for
just a short time, can be difficult. When I was a boy, my sentimental
dad would demand a hug practically every time I left the room. Now
a father myself, I understand what compelled his emotional excess.
I leave my children on a daily basis, often for many hours. They
are usually still asleep when I depart for work, and at times they are
done for the night before I return. Early in the morning, when they
are both snoozing soundly in their shared bed, limbs tangled like
human origami, I whisper a farewell in their ears and kiss them each
softly on their cheeks.

When I have the pleasure of bringing my daughter to school in
the morning, she hugs my leg tightly, tears in her brown eyes. "Papa,
I don't want you to go," she says between huffy, indignant sobs. It
always feels hard to leave her in these moments. Even though I want
her to grow to be more independent, I also yearn to hold on to this
sweet time of her youth for as long as possible. I like feeling needed
and necessary, because I know it will not always be this way.

"My love, I don't want to leave you either," I tell her with a soft
kiss on the crown of her head, "but I will be right here to pick you

up when school is done. Goodbye."

Goodbye. Usually when we utter this simple and common word, what we really mean to communicate—if we think about it much at all—is that I will see you later and I wish you well until I do. Then, we usually go about our day, assuming that this entreaty will be unconditionally met. The goodbyes that I have been a part of in the hospital are often permanent though, and, in those moments, the well-wish feels much more profound. These sad farewells have changed the way I feel about leaving my children every morning. They have changed the way I say goodbye to them.

Until I began the work I now do, death and dying were phenomena I associated primarily with the elderly—people who had already lived long lives. In this hospital though, I see children die. When they are gone, it is the nurses and sometimes their parents who care for their bodies. As we do so, we all must attempt to understand and accept that they are gone.

One day, while standing before the body of a deceased five-year-old child I had previously cared for, I half expected that he would suddenly open his eyes and smile at me. I felt this even though I saw him smile only once when he was alive. He had been giggling at a cartoon while distractedly nibbling on a piece of fruit, his mother cuddled beside him.

Most of the time though, he seemed in far too much pain for any kind of happiness. His name was Amar. His family had brought him all the way from Tibet in hopes of curing a tumor in his spine that ultimately could not be cured on any continent. Amar often cried out for God to take his life rather than endure any more pain. I did not understand what he had been saying until a troubled interpreter translated his pleas. When I grasped what Amar was communicating, my stomach seized with the sorrow of a fellow parent—a sensation I can only describe as suddenly speeding down a massive roller coaster.

Eventually, deep into the night, God granted Amar his wish. When his little body had been tortured enough, it surrendered to a disease that his heart and mind no longer had the will to fight against. His parents cuddled with him for many hours before they bathed his body. As was the custom of their culture, they then wrapped a traditional Buddhist cloth around him.

After they left, we gently placed Amar in the required hospital-issued body bag. His peaceful face peeked quietly out of the patterned folds of the delicate shroud that his parents had bundled around him, which was now swaddled by the bright-white bag. The vibrant green cloth—the tradition of his people—lay in stark contrast to the plastic and sterile-looking bag—the tradition of our morgue.

As we waited for an attendant to escort us and Amar's body downstairs, a small group of caretakers stood together around his bed: Cassi, Rebecca, Stephanie, Mark, and myself. We were just a few of the many people who took care of Amar when he was alive, and now that he was dead, we were still with him. Standing above the boy's body, we told each other lighthearted stories about him and his family—the few happy moments that punctuated all the other sad times.

Mark, the family's social worker, had been present at Amar's bedside since three that morning. Such dedication is not necessarily in his job description, but it is most certainly in his human description. That morning, Mark had a weariness to him that seemed to hang off his shoulders like a heavy cloak, but he was still smiling. He was still there.

Rebecca is tall and has long jet-black hair. When I see her in passing at work, each of us focused on a nursing task, she almost always pauses and asks, "Hey Buddy. You good?" Except for the many freckles and an often-goofy smile that populate her face, Rebecca looks a bit like a real-life Wonder Woman.

She was standing on the opposite side of Amar's bed. With some exasperation she looked at me and said, "Sometimes, I just can't believe what we do here every day. How do you explain this to people who don't see it?"

We purposely did not cover Amar's face. This would be the last time we would ever see him, and it felt wrong to shield his bearing from our view. I think that we didn't want him to feel lonely there in that plastic bag. In my head, I could hear the determined plea of his distraught mother who, hours earlier, had exacted a promise from Mark that her son would not be left alone after she had gone.

Just before we left with Amar's body on our slow walk to the morgue, I gently rubbed his head, which was now full of new dark hair. For the first time, I noticed his naturally sculpted eyebrows, which he inherited from the face of his kind mother. His eyelids, feathered with long and delicate lashes, were still ever so slightly open to the world and gazing vacantly at something that was not us.

Stephanie, a nurse who has three children of her own and often pines about having a fourth, gently massaged those eyelids shut in the instinctive manner of a mother tenderly putting her child to sleep. She zipped up the white bag. It occurred to me in that moment that not even death could steal the smooth beauty that graced Amar's face. Nor did his death disabuse me of the unrealistic expectation that he might, somehow, rise again.

The fanciful notion of resurrection usually makes little sense to me, but a dead child makes even less sense. Every time a child dies, my sense of order leaps out the window, leaving me back in the room and to my own devices to pick up the scattered pieces. This boy was barely five years old. His life had just begun. Even though he made it clear that he could no longer stand the pain, that his preference was to die, his family was not ready for him to go. The great pain and sorrow they openly expressed revealed that his death made as little sense to them as it did to us. It belied their spiritual convictions that his soul was amenable to moving on karmically to the next life. As one of Amar's nurses, it made me wonder what, if any, good had I ever really done him and his family.

The walk downstairs with Amar's body was calm and somber, like a memorial in motion. When we opened the large metal doors to the refrigerated section of the morgue, I instinctively withdrew from the invisible cloud of frigid air that quickly moved through the room. As this cool, manufactured current touched my body, the skin of my arms erupted into cities of tiny goosebumps. No matter how prepared I think I am, this same visceral reaction always overtakes me here in this cold, hollow space.

I tenderly picked up Amar's body and placed it down on the first available tray. It felt so much lighter than I expected it would. In that moment, my mind was transported back to the night before when I had picked up my own daughter, asleep in her pink nightgown, and placed her in bed. Her calm expression then and Amar's serene face now reminded me of the narrow distance between the repose of sleep and stillness of death.

As we all said goodbye to Amar, I remembered a time many years ago when I first went to the hospital morgue. That day, I was surprised to see that the locked room had no attendant. I had envisioned someone sitting there, quietly watching just in case God was not, but there was no one there. The bodies were all alone, stacked above and below their corporeal neighbors on long metal trays that slid soundlessly in and out. Who would take care of all these people? I had thought. Years later, I knew better than to expect such vigilance for our dead children. Their bodies would be alone.

Saying goodbye to a child who has died, no matter how many times I must do it, will never feel routine to me. I don't want it to feel normal. The solemn act has changed me and altered the way I relate to my own children. Although I may sometimes bid farewell to my own kids in haste—the ritual chaos of our daily lives almost demands it—I will never do so without purpose and presence. As I part from my children, I always try to lock eyes with them until they, distracted by the chaos of their friends and classrooms, look away first. I want to be present in that moment. I am always aware of what goodbyes mean to me and what my kids mean to me, too.

Shortly after he passed away, Amar's mother observed that her son had died on the same day of the week on which, over five years earlier, he had been born: a Wednesday. The temporal synchronicity of her son's birth and of his death brought her great comfort, she said. It was just one of the things she chose to hold on to as she said goodbye, too.

SHOWING UP FOR YOUR KIDS

You do these things; you don't process them. You move on to the next thing. You give, and you give, and you give because you want to and because you are constantly seeing it happen around you. That's what everybody is doing. Nobody is sitting around.

– Ashley, pediatric oncology nurse, mother

With such energetic and challenging children, I sometimes feel like I am failing as a father long before I have even begun. In those sad early morning moments when my patience is meager, my insights redundant, my humor nonexistent, and the level of caffeine in my bloodstream deficient, I remind myself that at least I'm there.

As my non-caffeinated kids perform a modified drag race through our kitchen, they yell, scream, laugh, bicker, cry, push, and pull at me and each other. They were wearing pajamas at the beginning of their improvised game, but they are now both much closer to naked. It is easier to feel wild when your skin touches the cold morning air. Amidst their complex game of learning to be humans and mine of learning to be a father, I rarely know the best words to say or the smartest actions to take. Within the numerous moments of laughter and love, which my children supply in a steady and unending stream, is a general feeling of bewildered ambivalence of what to do and how to be.

With the children I work with, I have also struggled to know what to say, do, or even feel. Here, I am often witness to very impactful news being delivered to a family regarding their child's health. Sometimes, this news is positive—a scan clear of cancer or a blood test indicating an unexpected benign result, and it is in these moments that I know how to act or be. It feels natural to celebrate for those on whom fortune has shone brightly. When the news is bad though, when a family learns that a cancer has returned and that there is nothing left to be done, I sometimes struggle with what to say and do. Even though I have been doing this work for over a decade and have grown accustomed to finding comfort in uncomfortable moments, I don't always know how to read a situation. It is simply not always clear. Forget about not knowing what to say or do, I sometimes even feel unsure about how to orient my body. Do I cross my arms over my chest or let them rest at my side? Do I offer physical comfort? Do I initiate a caring embrace?

What I have learned is that every difficult situation is unique. As a nurse and as a parent, there is no prescribed formula for how I should navigate the bumps. What was an effective technique one day may fall flat the next day. In the face of such uncertainty, the best I can do is be sincere, present, and available. Simply showing up is the most important part.

It was late in the day, in the middle of winter. The solstice was not far off and it was already dark outside. I was at work, standing in the doc box—the small room where the doctors work and run patient rounds. This is the place where patient care plans are hatched, lab results are interpreted, and also where young doctors learn how to care for very sick children. They learn from more experienced physicians, and often from the nurses who, in many ways, know these kids and their parents the best.

Passing by this space, a casual observer may peek inside to see doctors typing away at various workstations or in focused conversation with their colleagues. A giant white board features, in rough alphabetical order, the contact numbers to every service in the hospital: IMMUNOLOGY, IP3...ORTHO, PACU, PATHOLOGY. Next to that sits a door that leads to the main nursing station. During the busier parts of the day, this door is in near constant use by the blue blur of the nursing staff as they enter and exit in order to interface with the doctors on behalf of their young patients.

At this moment though, the room was mostly empty. Most of the computers were sleeping. Nobody was coming or going. A pink cardboard pastry box lay seductively open on a pile of lab papers. It contained a lone half-eaten croissant with a colorful drape of crumbs surrounding it, suggesting its former doughy compatriots.

It was about 6:30 p.m.—not a common or convenient time for the delivery of important news, good or bad, but the news had found us anyway. I was standing there with two doctors. We all looked at each other, a pregnant pause occupying our space. The pathology lab had just delivered the preliminary results for a teenage boy. The results were not good, but also not surprising. After almost two years of various therapies, the boy's bone marrow was still packed full of leukemia cells. There were no remaining options for him.

Both the physicians who were standing before me have an impressive mastery of this complex field of medicine. They are also both very down-to-earth and compassionate people. Although neither of them has kids of their own, they know how to talk to children by not talking down to them. If my own kids ever became seriously ill, I would want these doctors taking care of them. There was so much to be said in that moment that a question seemed the most appropriate way to begin.

"Should we tell them now? Or wait for conclusive results in the morning?" asked Amit, the attending physician.

Of all the doctors I work with, Amit is one of my favorites. He has prominent features and thick dark hair. Always impeccably dressed and groomed, he is not afraid of mixing bold pastels under his crisp white physician lab coat. Amit possesses a gentle way of engaging with the world. He has the innate gift of being able to communicate information, good or bad, in a way that sets his patients and their parents at ease. It is clear he cares. He and Ashley, the fellow physician that day, both looked at me with questioning expressions as if I should know the answer. Even though I'd spent hundreds of hours with this boy and his mother over the course of his illness, I was also unsure.

The teenage boy was Ben. Each morning when I was assigned to care for him, I sat with his mom Jaclyn for a few minutes on one side of the couch she had slept on the night prior. We talked in hushed voices about the medical plan for that day and any concerns or questions she had. We chatted about whatever was on her mind too, and sometimes about what was on mine. Sometimes, I surprised myself with the extent of intimate details I shared with this woman in those quiet moments. Jaclyn was equally as forthcoming. We were both parents with a common yet diverging experience. My kids were just beginning their lives; everything was new for them and for me as a dad. Ben, sensitive and wise, was on the brink of adulthood, quietly contemplating the reality that he would not make it there; Jaclyn watched, not yet ready to accept that fate. I wondered silently why my kids had been spared the pain and hurt that Ben was experiencing, and if they would always be so lucky.

The friendly relationship I shared with Jaclyn was built upon regular dialogue in which little was concealed. Just by being herself—a lovely and committed mother who was always there—Jaclyn taught me so much. As much as I mourn Ben's absence from this world, I also miss seeing and talking to his mom as much as I once did. She reminds me of a slightly younger version of my own mother, without the parental baggage, of course. We are still friends. Occasionally, we go for long hikes together. As we navigate the winding trails, we, of course, talk about her son. He is what binds us together. We talk about our present lives too—my daily travails as a parent, as well as her constant reality: what it is like to be a parent of a boy no longer living.

As I pondered Amit's question, I tried to imagine what it would feel like to be on the receiving end of such news. The power of magical thinking and sheer hope in the face of such grim possibilities can be startling. It is possible to believe in the impossible, even when every fact before you runs counter to that belief.

"The results are real," I finally muttered to Amit. "We don't want to believe it, of course, but we all know it, right?" My voice sounded unsure, even to me.

"Yes," said Amit, and then he looked to the space on the floor between his feet. His pursed lips hung like a sad prop below his strong of-another-era moustache. "The pathologist I talked to saw nothing but cancer cells when she was looking in the microscope."

"Well then, they deserve to hear it from us, and they should hear it now," I said. "We are the people who know them the best. I don't think there's a difference between a sleepless night or a worry-ridden day for Jaclyn. She won't be sleeping much tonight anyway."

"You're right. Thanks for being our moral compass today," replied Amit. I cringed when he said it. Even though I had not been seeking his validation, I was embarrassed by how much I relished it from a colleague who I respected so much. My vanity aside, I knew that I cared about these two people and I wanted to be in the room with them when they heard the news. I knew it would be unpleasant, but they needed to know. Looking back, I think what Amit really meant to thank me for was my willingness to voice what we all knew to be true, that this boy was going to die soon.

"I can do the talking," said Ashley, sadly. "I feel like I have never given these two anything but bad news anyway."

It was true. Ever since the initial diagnosis that brought him back home a month after starting college, Ben had been fighting an uphill battle. The hill slowly transformed into a mountain. I had been sensing lately that he was ready to stop fighting. He was a soft-spoken boy, but his clear, intelligent eyes always spoke volumes to me. Lately, those tired eyes said, I'm done. I was not aware of it, but months earlier Ben had admitted to one of his most trusted doctors that he was ready to go. That he was only holding on for his parents. "I am going to keep going on for a while—for them," he told her.

After a deep collective breath, we headed for their hospital room. Amit knocked softly on the door. I don't remember everything that went said and unsaid in that room; I was nervous to be occupying such an intimate space with such sensitive news. The doctors did most of the talking anyway. I do remember being at the foot of Ben's bed, unsure of how to stand.

Everything felt awkward. Even feeling awkward felt awkward. It was so different than I usually felt around this mom and her son. I do remember that the news was delivered compassionately, but in a way that was unambiguous. There was little else to offer him now other than our own sadness and options to relieve Ben's physical pain.

Despite that, Jaclyn immediately began negotiating with this expected yet unbelievable reality. She asked questions of the doctors for which there were no answers: "What now? What do we do next?" She desperately wanted to do something, anything, even as she was told that there was nothing left to do.

Ben was shirtless and sitting up in his bed. His skin was ghostly pale, and his hair, which had once been dark and lush, was now reduced to fuzzy isolated islands on his head. The pillow behind him was littered with curly follicles that had newly fallen during the day. Because of the many awful sores that populated his mouth and throat, he had trouble speaking above a whisper. As Ashley spoke, Ben said nothing. He stared straight ahead, occasionally looking over at his mom who was sitting close by. Ben always watched out for his mom.

When Ashley was finished talking, she asked Ben if he had any questions for us. His face was almost expressionless. After a long pause, he said, "No...I'm good," in the same manner of a diner responding to a waiter who had just asked him if he needed a refill on his water.

Ben died in his sleep a few weeks later. I had been his nurse the day before he passed away. That evening, it was not obvious to me that he would die just fourteen hours later.

Before I left his hospital room that night I said, "Goodbye, you two. I will see you in a few days," just like I had said so many times before.

His family held Ben's memorial service at a park they had frequented often when he was young. Jaclyn had asked me to speak a few words on behalf of all the nurses who had loved and taken care of Ben.

As I stood at the podium, my young son was sleeping against my chest in a carrier. I needed him close to me. I told a story about Ben. It was a story that exemplified the kind of person I thought he was—his calm presence, his unique ease with the world and his disease. I was close to tears as I told it. My son was snoring.

When I was done talking, the audience was silent. I locked eyes with Ben's mom who was sitting in the front row a few feet away. In that moment, it felt like the hundreds of people in attendance had disappeared. It was just her and me.

"I'm so sorry," I said to her through sniffles and tears. "I should have been there when he died. I wanted to be there for you." It had not been my plan to address Ben's mom so directly, especially in front of so many people, but I was used to speaking with her frankly and without artifice. It was an impulsive act that simply felt like the right, most authentic thing to do.

There are other times, though, when the right thing to say or do is not clear. It feels the hardest to show up in those unsure moments. Recently, while eating lunch in the hospital cafeteria, I ran into Beth, the mother of a former patient named Rachel.

During Rachel's treatment, I had gotten to know her and her family well, but I had not seen them for quite a while. Ostensibly, Rachel had achieved remission from her disease and was back to her normal life.

By now, I am used to that familiar sinking feeling when I see a family back in the hospital after a long absence. When our patients leave the hospital for the last time, we truly hope to never see them again. We want them out there in the world enjoying life—making mistakes and learning from them, succeeding, failing, laughing, crying, and doing all the things that kids growing into themselves do. We want to hear about these things, not directly from them, but tangentially and from a distance. Send a Christmas card with your smiling family in front of the tree. No cancer, please.

There even exists a very real pediatric oncology nursing taboo that decrees that the name of patients cured and in remission should never be mentioned out loud. This practice, like Harry Potter's reluctance to mention Voldemort's name in fear of conjuring his evil, is taken very seriously by some of my colleagues. I don't believe in it too much and my big mouth often gets me into trouble. My colleagues often shush me when I begin to reminisce about a past patient whom we have not seen for a long while.

When I first saw Beth, my first inclination was to avoid speaking to her. I felt that hopeless feeling in my gut and that familiar fear of not having the right words to comfort. As I stood there, contemplating my shoes and all the shitty unfairness in the world, I silently pleaded to the universe that she and Rachel were here for another reason other than the most obvious one. A checkup maybe? A nostalgic visit to the hospital cafeteria?

I looked up. Beth was standing right in front of me. I could tell from her red eyes that she had just been crying. She looked like she had just rolled out of bed. The bottom button on her thin blue cardigan was inserted awkwardly into the wrong buttonhole, her plaid shirt tail sticking out from the bottom.

"Rachel's cancer is back," she told me plainly and without further explanation. It was the same cancer Rachel had when she was younger. She was a week shy of starting her freshman year in high school.

I really like Rachel. She is artistic and generously delivers smiles or giggles. She was learning to play the guitar when I last saw her and she loves to dance. She used to give me regular updates on the cute things her pocketbook puppy had been up to. If my daughter were her age, they would be fast friends.

As I caught up with Beth, we fell into the familiar rhythm of conversation we used to have. I knew she felt anxious in the hospital, and she seemed to always appreciate it when we could talk something out. Even though she was clearly weary and distraught, she seemed eager to tell me what was happening with her little girl.

It can be difficult to know what to say to a person who has received such bad news. In reality though, I think that this is generally my difficulty and not at all theirs.

A mother of a child who tragically died of a chronic disease once said, "You can always talk to me about my child. I might cry and get upset, but it's not as if I suddenly forgot about him and you reminded me. I think about him every day. It's okay if I cry. It's okay if I get upset. I will, but I would love for you to ask me about him. I would love to share stories about him."

I often think about this mother's words when I need to be there for a parent or a child when they are at their lowest. It is true with my own kids as well. I have learned that words are important, and when the sentiments are sincere and heartfelt, they can have great power. After almost a decade of such cafeteria encounters and innumerable moments in which my own kids have confronted me with their own issues, I have found that dancing around these sensitive topics is awkward and unhelpful. When I saw Beth, I said exactly what I felt in that moment, hoping that I was reading her needs correctly.

"I am really so sorry to hear about this. Rachel is such a lovely and amazing person. She does not deserve any of this. And you are such a great mother, Beth. She is lucky to have you and such a strong supportive family to help her through this. We will do anything we can do to make this time easier for you. I am so sorry that you have to go through this all again, but I am happy to be able to see you."

It was all true. I just had to show up to say it.

BREAK FROM THE HEARTBREAK
THE GHOST FART

Our job has so much heaviness, but there is such a lightness too. No matter how heavy it is, we can come up with something to laugh about in the break room.

– Allie, pediatric oncology nurse, baby kisser

Kate, a fellow nurse, told me a story that reminded me of the incredible amount of levity, humor, and transcendence from pain that sometimes exists here. The stories we share may be sad, but they are not always bleak.

Kate, who has bright-blue eyes and a freckled nose, often dons a thick white sweater over her scrubs. She is not good at hiding her emotions. Her revealing face betrays any attempt at psychological compartmentalization. You can see it in her smile. It is a complicated expression that seems both happy and melancholic at the same time. Her patients see this too. They trust her with their pain and with their joy as well.

"It was always a funny room," recalled Kate, as she described the general vibe of a particular teenage boy she cared for often. "You would be laughing all the time when you were in there." She was working the night shift at that point in her career and, by her own acknowledgement, her stomach "did not do well on night shift."

"I was super gassy and I fucking farted in the room. It was silent and it was smelly."

Most people are familiar with this particular silent yet deadly phenomena that is conveniently quiet, yet still very much detectable. Even among the many pungent aromas of the hospital, Kate admitted that this fart stood out.

Unfortunately, the smell woke her patient and his father, who was sleeping across the room. As Kate finished collecting her labs in the still, dark room, it did not take long for the boy and his father to engage in a comical dialogue about the source of the smell that had woken them.

"Dad, did you just fucking fart?" the boy asked with an accompanying giggle in the dark.

"No," said his father, "I was asleep."

"No, you totally fucking farted in your sleep," accused the son. It was serious now.

"I didn't fart. It was you," his dad retorted.

"I didn't fart, Dad. I would have known if had farted."

"Well, I think it was your nurse," joked the dad. He particularly enjoyed causing Kate, a nurse he knew well, to blush, even if it was too dark for him to see her fair cheeks quickly turn a rosy hue.

"No, eww! I would never do that. You boys are so gross," declared Kate in a futile effort to dismiss the subject, even as the pungent smell continued to make its slow tour around the room until it faded away. But this was no ordinary gas. This flatus, in its own peculiar way, would rise again.

About two weeks later, this boy, who had cancer and a fantastic sense of humor, died unexpectedly of a fungal infection secondary to his disease. Although still technically a teenager, Kate remembers, he was really more like a man. When he was alive, he towered over most other people when he stood.

"He was a tall, big-boned teddy bear who, even when he felt like crap, would say thank you," she told me with her sad smile.

When he died, Kate was not at work, but she went to the hospital to be with his parents, to help bathe and take care of their son's body.

Before she and a few other nurses brought him down to the morgue, his mom looked at her and said, "Kate, don't leave his side. Please, I don't want him to be alone."

Weeks later, Kate, who does not typically go to many of her patient's funerals, attended this one. She loved this boy and his family. She knew it would mean a lot to them if she was there. When the service concluded, she gave the dead boy's mother a long hug, and afterward, she hugged his father as well. He hugs just like his son did, she thought to herself in his arms, like a big, cuddly bear.

As the suffering man embraced her, he whispered slowly into her ear. "Kate, I know it was you who farted that night."

Blushing once again, Kate pulled away and replied with an indignant smile that I can easily picture on her freckled face: "I can't believe you just called me out for farting. It's your son's funeral!"

The father answered back with a laugh that was also a cry. "It was totally you. That was a nasty one."

YOUR PARTNER IS YOUR BEST PARTNER

I have seen plenty of situations which show the evil of cancer and the anger it can create. That is where tolerance comes into it all—respecting the difference and respecting that anger.

- Rob, pediatric oncology attending physician, father

I vividly remember the first really big fight that my wife and I had as a couple, even if I don't recall the circumstances that started it. In its aftermath, though, we were sitting as far away from each other as our compact couch allowed. My arms were crossed tightly over my chest. I remember feeling so vulnerable and angry at the same time.

She was looking down at her feet. They were clad in a pair of cotton socks adorned with designs of grinning dinosaurs. Not willing to meet her eyes, I stared at those socks too, wondering what in the world could make a T-Rex so happy. Then, I met her tearful glance, and began to wonder what in the world could make the woman I adored so sad (me).

"You need to kiss me when I'm sad like this," she then told me.

"What if it's me who's making you so sad?" I mumbled back.

"In that case, kiss me even more," she responded.

With that witty retort, the ice in my heart melted. I remembered that this woman loved me, even if she didn't always agree with me. That she always wanted the best for me, even if she did not always quite know what that was. That she was funny, smart, and compassionate.

I crossed the continent of the couch between us and kissed her lightly on the cheek. Our fight was suddenly over, and the way we resolved it provided a roadmap for how we might resolve many future moments of relationship strife.

We did not have children then. We were happily unaware of how the stress of parenthood would often cause discord in our future relationship. We were only just beginning to understand how we might navigate all the hard times that are part of loving another person.

I could not imagine embarking on this challenge of parenting without my wife as my partner. We back each other up. When that dreaded witching hour transforms our two reasonable children into, well, witches, we are both there to calm the witch and the warlock down, read them books, and get them to bed.

I need her. My lovely wife makes subtle suggestions about how I might deepen my connection with one of my kids—thoughtful gestures that would never even occur to me.

She needs me. I take the heat off a burgeoning tiff between my hotheaded daughter and her frustrated mom by staging a silly impromptu dance party in the kitchen. No audible music required.

Even though we depend on each other to make it through the hardest parts of parenting (and to enjoy the fun parts, too), we still manage to hurt each other. Often. When my discerning wife questions one of my admittedly questionable parenting moves, I sometimes take it as criticism of myself as a person. I feel deflated instead of supported. When I feel overwhelmed by all the screaming, fighting, and whining in our home, I sometimes give up. I retreat, leaving my wife alone with the chaos that is our children.

She feels abandoned. But because life has been so good to us—our children are healthy, we are healthy—we always recover from these disagreements. We always find a way to grow and move forward together. Sometimes, all it takes is a subtle, well-placed phrase.

In the hospital, routine disagreements can expand, explode, and ultimately destroy a couple. It is here—where relationships are both built and broken—that I have learned how important having a partner in parenthood is. Too many times, I have felt like a fly on the wall, trying to act invisible as two scared, tired, and angry parents tear each other apart, picking on each other for otherwise excusable character faults, that, in the moment, seem bigger and brighter than a harvest moon.

"You're not doing it right!" hissed the mom of a little boy I was taking care of one day.

Her vitriol was directed not at me, but rather at the boy's dad, an affable, harmless-looking man who was doing his best with all thumbs to extract their hysterical toddler from the puke-stained onesie and blanket wrapped around him.

Her comment was meant as a provocation rather than an offer of help. She stood in the corner of the hospital room, as far away from the chaos as she could get, her arms folded tightly to her chest as if she didn't want to be contaminated by anything. Her posture seemed to say *Stay away from me* before she even opened her mouth.

Her husband, teeth gritted in frustration and visibly sweating, was fumbling over his son, but really only making the situation worse. The baby's onesie was emblazoned with the words I love Grandma in the front, but that hopeful declaration was now obscured by a large splat of vomit. His outfit was incomprehensibly wrapped around the many infusion lines that sprouted from the IV pole next to the bed and ended in sites on both his arm and chest. Squirming around on the sheets, he looked like a messy plate of spaghetti.

His mom, still not helping, glowered menacingly from the corner of the room. "I don't even know why you bother coming to the hospital," she said to her husband. "You're not helping."

As I stood there, uncomfortably witnessing this display of spousal strife, I wondered when it would be appropriate to insert myself. I stepped in to aid this hapless dad in untangling his boy, hoping that my neutral presence would diffuse the bad vibes in the room or, at the very least, subdue them.

However, even as we worked together to wash the young boy, his angry mom continued to berate her husband, not caring that I was in the room. "Worthless. Worthless," she muttered down at her shoes.

As she paced her side of the room like a caged tiger, it was hard for me to imagine that she had ever even smiled. There must have been carefree times before their son had cancer, times when these two people actually liked and treated each other well, but it was not apparent. I spoke in soft, encouraging tones to the little boy as I removed his soiled garment and washed his sticky body.

My calm voice was meant for him, but also for his dad who, by that time, had collapsed defeatedly into a chair next to the bed. Still holding his son's hand, he closed his eyes and rested his forehead softly on the pillow in front of him.

His son was breathing heavily from the exertion of the tantrum that had precipitated his massive puke. The small yellow tube that had been inserted into his nostril for the administration of formula and medicines pushed out and then retracted back into his nostril along with each labored huff. He slipped his thumb into his mouth and began methodically sucking.

His mom, her pacing ceased, no longer mumbled to herself. She stood silently like a statue, covering her face with her two slender, manicured hands. I noticed on the ring finger of her left hand a large diamond snuggled against a more modest gold wedding band. Under the harsh halo of the overhead lights, the center jewel glimmered like a solitary star in an otherwise cold and dark night sky. Their son ultimately survived, but I don't know if his parents' marriage did.

In another hospital room, years earlier, a young girl was suffering from a cancer called neuroblastoma. This disease is rare, and the prognosis is grim. Even when we manage to push it into remission, it often returns.

This young girl was clearly dying, and although both her parents were deeply involved in her care, the manner in which they each coped with her imminent death was very different, causing a great deal of distress in their marriage.

Her mother had a strong Christian background and she clung to her faith like a life raft in a stormy sea. Her father was an atheist. He did not believe his daughter would be heading to heaven and he was frustrated by what he saw as his wife's naive beliefs. He loved his daughter deeply, but he refused to find solace in what he saw as a fairytale. His wife was pained because he did not share her more hopeful beliefs that their daughter's soul would travel on and that they would someday see her again.

They argued back and forth as their sick daughter lay sleeping. The girl's father could sometimes be heard saying loudly to his wife, "THERE IS NO FUCKING HEAVEN."

While no relationship is free of strife or discontent, it is easy to see how the serious illness of a child can disrupt even the strongest ones. It is the hard and challenging moments in life, not the fun times, that expose the true integrity of the bonds between two people. Whether it is one parent cruelly critiquing her partner as he does his best to take care of their sick child, a father angrily haranguing his spouse over her need for salvation, or me checking out when times are hard with my own kids, these behaviors are motivated by our desire to feel understood and safe. To feel loved.

Just as I have seen people lose their relationships to the fear and sadness caused by the sickness or death of a child, I have also witnessed two people managing to sustain and grow their love, despite such circumstances. Such love has become a model for me.

There was one particular set of parents who, it appeared to me, were always able to make their situation feel better, despite how bad it actually became. They were young parents, much younger than me, and their deep love for each other was clear to anybody who saw them together. They had a gentle way of looking at each other that without words just said, I adore you.

This obvious affection was second only to their devotion to Nathan, their young boy. They rarely left each other's side during many months of waiting for good, but in their case, often bad news. These times were punctuated by numerous, life-threatening moments. I, myself, sent Nathan down to the pediatric ICU twice when his care could no longer be managed safely by our oncology team.

During all this time, however, these two people always nurtured their relationship with each other. I know that this required a great deal of diligence, patience, and trust on their part. They experienced so many hard times that surely challenged their love, but they somehow made it look effortless.

There was a hospital bed in their room, but it was rarely used. As I tiptoed into their space in the morning to check Nathan's vital signs, I almost always found them, these three players in this family band, cuddled together on a large inflatable bed, which rested on the floor. They were two exhausted parents with their snoring son lying between them. The IV pole next to the bed trailed medication lines that wound around them, between legs, and under backs, but always found their way to that small boy. This was their life. This was their family, and for a time, they made this place their home.

Allie, a nurse colleague of mine, who is a self-identified baby kisser and not ashamed of it, made a thoughtful observation about these two parents. "They were such a strong couple," she recalled. "I would ask if they wanted me to hold their son for a while and they would always say yes. I would hold him, and they would embrace each other for ten minutes and just cry together. I think it is the sign of a good relationship when you are still able to lean on each other during times with bad news instead of just holding on to your kids who you could potentially lose. I would think that some parents would just want to hold on to him and hold on to him, but they wanted and needed each other too."

Observing the way these two were so seamlessly connected and aware of each other's needs made me wish that every couple with a sick child could summon the time and patience to care for each other as they did, but I know this is simply not always possible. I understand how the stress and fear of a child's illness can cause a rift in a relationship, but I can also appreciate how maintaining that love and understanding is so important to healing that same pain.

After a long struggle with his disease, Nathan died. We just couldn't save him. He came to us as an infant and left us as a toddler. Despite the great loss that these two parents experienced, it seemed to me that their love for each other only grew stronger over time.

NURTURE THE BONDS BETWEEN YOUR CHILDREN

When a patient is at the end of life, I appreciate when their siblings are in the room. I try to make parents aware of the fact that as much as they think they may be scaring the other kid, he or she will appreciate it later on.

– Allie, pediatric oncology nurse

From my birth to about the age of three, my place of sleep was a bulky white 1970s-style crib. Constrained as I was behind the wooden (possibly lead-painted) bars, I remember staring into an identical crib that held my baby brother. Each and every night, one year in age and a few feet in air separated us. When the lights were out but we were not, my brother and I partook in semi-babbling dialogues to pass the time until we finally fell asleep.

Eventually, we both graduated to our own twin beds, and that is when the real trouble began. My brother was a sleepwalker, and without the bars of the crib holding him back, he rarely stayed in bed for long. He walked.

One night, my mom woke up to find him standing over her bed with an apple in one hand and a paring knife in the other. "Cut it," he mumbled to her. He was completely asleep and apparently hungry for fruit.

Another time, my brother and I managed to flood our entire carpeted bedroom by shoving socks into the drain of a running sink. I do not recall the motivation for this bit of naughtiness, but the result was a wet and moldy carpet and some mighty pissed-off parents. Until the screaming began, my brother and I were absolutely thrilled by our homemade slip-and-slide.

I have slept in many beds since that time. One was lofted above a desk where I often sat shirtless, sincerely composing bad poetry. Both the loft and the poetry made me feel pretty cool at the time. In a later bed, an insect colony of the bedbug variety lived quite happily until they found themselves out on the curb, along with their mattress home.

These days, life has dictated yet another bed change. I am part of a family of four and, despite my wife's and my desire for some alone time, we often have a family bed.

Once our second child was born, we made the very adultlike decision to update our sleeping situation to an amazing king-size bed. I was not used to such a spacious sleeping arrangement. So vast is our new bed, I often feel like I am snoozing on top of Iowa. Sometimes, deep into the night, I find myself performing a modified snow angel just to determine if my sleeping wife is still beside me. When we were young, more beautiful, and unsaddled by children, this maneuver was unnecessary. Our bed—a full size—was just what we needed, and allowed for lots of touchy-feely closeness with minimal snow angel reconnaissance.

Alas, our new bed is also a veritable zoo populated by four: a chubby monkey, a Tasmanian devil, and the two zookeepers, otherwise known as Mama and Papa. I love having my children close to me at night. I love hearing their nighttime breathing, so effortless and intermittently interrupted by sweet little coughs and harmless tooty farts. My son sleeps with his two hands resting beneath his head as if, in his dreams, he is tanning on some bright and foreign beach. He often ends up sleeping sideways between my wife and I, transforming us all for a time in to one big sleeping "H."

Home, Hugs, Happy.

My daughter is more complicated than her carefree brother. Like me, she mercilessly grinds her teeth in her sleep. Her dream mind seems to be crowded with creepy crawly things and existential concerns that only an imaginative five-year-old could conjure up. She often wakes up screaming about something in her dreams that we cannot begin to fathom or protect her from. All we can do is hold her and sing her back to sleep.

One night, she did manage to describe to me what scared her awake at three in the morning. It was abejas (bees), she told me, "flying all around and stinging" her. My daughter dreams in Spanish, talks in Spanglish, and whines in English. It is all adorable except for the whining part.

My kids—these two little souls—are so different from each other and yet so similar too. I see daily, through their goofy interactions, how they change and grow. These two troublemakers are a team. Their relationship will be one of the most important connections they will ever have. I see it happening already. She patiently translates his jumbled monologues for strangers to understand. When she is sad or angry, he cuddles with her like a goofy teddy. She quietly talks him down from the heights of his most intransigent, parent-wrecking tantrums. He causes her to giggle uncontrollably just by being his natural silly self.

I have two brothers. We were all born within three years of each other (my parents must have had a small bed at first too). The man I am today is in large part due to the influence of my brothers. We laughed, we played, we cried, and, despite a few very regretful rock fights and out-of-window tossings, we survived into adulthood intact and eager to seize the world.

I am sure I would have still made it this far if I had been an only child, but I would probably be a bit more boring and a lot less prepared to tackle the challenges life has to offer. Brothers are like scabs—the initial experience can be painful and bloody, but through that process your skin gets tougher and you learn to deal with the bumps that life brings. Adversity makes us stronger, and so do aggressive brothers.

Despite our best efforts to be there for our pediatric patients—to support them emotionally and psychologically—there often exists a chasm between us. Even their parents, who know their kids better than anyone, are at times unable to connect with their child in ways they are accustomed to. Their child is different than they were prior to diagnosis. They are altered. Their bodies are sometimes transformed in ways that make them virtually unrecognizable. Their minds—shocked by the trauma of the hospital experience and the effects of therapy—operate in new ways and with new emotional and intellectual parameters. It can be challenging for many parents to know how to connect with this new version of their child.

Their younger siblings, however, are often able to cross this bridge. By virtue of their age and their innocence, they have fewer expectations for what is normal and thereby are more adaptable.

An eight-year-old boy had just returned to his hospital room after undergoing a brain biopsy procedure that had sadly confirmed the presence of a malignant tumor. The energy in the room was sad; his parents remained quiet and solemn. So mournful were the room's occupants that it seemed almost like the walls themselves should be weeping. The funereal stillness was interrupted only by his mother periodically stepping out of the room in order to cry away from her son.

The boy sat in his bed fully awake, but he was so withdrawn that Kate, the nurse caring for him that day, wondered if his taciturn demeanor might be a neurological symptom of his disease progression. More likely, she thought, he was simply beginning to understand the gravity of his situation. She had known him to be a kind and gentle boy, but the trauma of the hospital had turned him a bit stoic and removed.

Several hours later, into the grim silence skipped his sweet, soft-spoken little sister. She was half his age and, when he saw her, the boy's face lit up like it was Christmas morning.

Without saying a word and with little hesitation, this little girl with blonde hair and freckles crawled into her brother's bed and lay beside him. She showed no fear or trepidation for the sterile strangeness of the hospital or the large, scary incision on her brother's head. She was here to see her best friend and she had brought her favorite stuffy to keep him company. The two kids quietly snuggled up to each other, head to head, sharing a loving stare that communicated in a language only they were fluent in.

Kate told me that it was as if the little girl spoke to him only with her eyes, saying, I know you're sad. I know you're scared. Everyone else is scared too, but I am here for you. The moment was filled with the pure love of a sibling who had brought a sense of short-lived normalcy to an abnormal place.

It is sometimes overlooked that the sisters and brothers of our patients—the people who they may feel the most emotionally connected to—take a perilous journey of their own. These kids also suffer the twists and turns of an uncertain roller coaster. In truth, siblings of chronically ill or dying children are subjected to profoundly difficult situations that they sometimes must navigate on their own. Simply because these children are spared from the disease that their siblings endure does not mean that they too are not saddled with a diagnosis. They carry the burden of being a healthy child, but they also must learn how to live with a disease. These kids suffer their own ailments of the heart and soul that are often unseen and unheard.

As their sibling is immersed in illness, and their parents concentrate all their energy in that direction, they might be left to their own devices for months and sometimes years. They may feel guilty for being the healthy one. Often, these kids harbor anger and resentment because their parents simply do not have the emotional and physical resources to properly care for them. They may develop feelings of depression, guilt, and serious emotional pathologies of their own as a consequence of the all-encompassing illness in their family.

Janine, the mother of a patient who I grew close to, told me that her longest stay in the hospital with James, her very sick toddler, was exactly 240 continuous days. For the first two months of that time, she was unable to see his older brother, who was only three years old at the time.

When I asked her how that sudden and extreme separation had affected Adam, her healthy son, she told me with some sadness and a straight face, "Well, he is a psycho now because of it. It was really hard for him, the worst thing ever for him. He did not get to see his mother for months; someone he was so attached to. Three years old is a difficult age. He was having anger issues. He started saying stuff about shooting and killing people. He got really socially fucked up from all of this."

Janine began to cry softly, and the pitch of her voice rose several decibels as she described the impact of her time away on her relationship with Adam. "It's definitely damaged, you know. We used to be so close and now he rebels and repels me. He's sort of cruel. He has these characteristics that before I would always nip in the bud, but they were so deeply ingrained after eight months of me constantly not being there. I lost control of that child. I could only focus on one. My other child was neglected, and his emotional needs were not met.

"To this day, I don't think we are quite there yet. I feel like if I had kept my control the whole time, he would be a different person. If I kept our rules in place—our tightness, our closeness—he would be in a better situation. One time, he was breaking down and saying, 'I want my family back. Mommy, I want my family back!' It was really sad. To hear a three-year-old say that is so hard."

Janine tried to describe to me what their life was like before her youngest son's illness, and how close her boys had been. "Before this," she began with a longing smile, "I used to take both kids to the park every day. We would eat lunch and hang out with other children. They would get good social interaction. They could go to the library one day a week for toddler time—activities that were done together as a family. But then everything just changed. No more parks, no more swings, no more slides, no more friends, no more social interactions. For [Adam], that had a lot to do with his anger. His whole life was transformed, and he still hasn't gotten it back."

I can understand what this kind of sibling deprivation would do to the equilibrium of even the most well-adjusted child. If my daughter were suddenly not allowed to see her little brother for an indeterminate amount of time, her world would be turned upside down. My kids depend on each other in ways that are still a mystery. They have formed an exclusive club of two that is currently accepting no new members.

I feel so lucky to have two children who are so familiar with each other and so unfamiliar with the inside of a hospital, who don't routinely take medicines in the morning and night, and who are free to explore this wonderful world without fear of getting sick from it. Both my kids have been playing around in the dirt together and poking around at bugs and snails since before they learned how to crawl. They have permanently dirty knees. This makes me happy.

Similarly, there is no five-second rule in our home. My son has an extreme Cheerio fixation. I often find him underneath the table foraging for lost and forgotten breakfast treasures. He cannot be stopped.

We may have a bit looser household than some, but our reality, whether it is scouring for half-stale breakfast cereal on the floor or rolling around in a wide field of grass, allows our kids to fully experience the world around them, and to fully experience each other.

As my kids interact unhindered with all the gifts this world provides, it is truly amazing to see their reactions and impressions. When they do it together, as partners, the experience is even richer. I hope it becomes one small patch of memory in the larger quilt of their lives together.

Kids learn so much about themselves through the words and actions of their brothers and sisters. They push each other's buttons and pull each other's levers. They learn what to model themselves after and perhaps what to avoid. They become allies carrying a common thread and, hopefully, a healthy and humorous perspective about those crazy fucking people they call Mama and Papa.

This togetherness—this closeness—is important. These bonds help to heal. I see it every day. Children who are ripped apart may also come back together. It never fails to surprise me how adaptable and strong these kids can be when they have each other. You can throw all types of horrible and rotten trauma at them, yet somehow they still move forward; they still overcome.

Adam, the young boy who was acting out during his mom's long absence, has come a long way since their family was reunited. In the early months of his brother's illness, I saw how he could be aggressive and combative, but he was also funny, energetic, and entertaining. Janine, his mom, was thrilled to tell me that her firecracker of a son is much healed from that uncertain time.

"He once told one of the doctors that he was going to flush him down the toilet, which I personally thought was hilarious," she said. "He does not say violent things to the nurses anymore. He would say that he was going to shoot them and that he was going to cut them with a knife—very aggressive things. These days, his interactions with the healthcare workers are not bad like that. He doesn't feel like they are taking his brother away from him anymore."

Long after they left the hospital, I visited James, Adam, and Janine on their home turf, and what I saw there was heartening and hopeful. Here were two boys—one still in the process of healing his mind and body, and the other working on mending his heart and soul. It was a joy to observe. They were screaming, rolling, laughing, and yelling. As Janine and I sat together, talking in her kitchen, it was all we could do to hear each other over their ruckus. As we chatted, she occasionally yelled lovingly at her older son to be gentler with his little brother so he would not accidentally (or on purpose) rip out his central line or nasogastric tube. In spite of the medical hardware, these two boys were once again creating a shared paradigm. It will belong to them and them alone. They are brothers.

Their relationship reminds me of the way my own son and daughter fight and play. I take joy in watching them form a special relationship that will also be their very own. I hope that they too create and share a private language that only they comprehend, and that they build experiences known only to them. I want these secrets to belong just to them. This is how they learn to love, and how I learn to let go.

BREAK FROM THE HEARTBREAK
CODE BROWN

To be able to laugh off the ridiculousness at work is one of the best parts of our job. It helps relieve the tension and nervous energy.

- Kirsten, pediatric oncology nurse

It is the cruel but expected fate of a father of two young children that I must deal with poop other than my own on a daily, sometimes hourly, basis. Before I had kids, I had no inkling how many times I would view and clean my son's anus. He must be under the impression that pooping will one day be accepted as an official event for the 2032 Olympics. He poops about six times a day as part of his intense and vigorous daily training regimen for this future athletic event.

With him, each diaper change is part marathon and part Greco-Roman wrestling. He fights, screams, and twists away from every wipe and tuck I attempt. He, too, has dared to scream "No, Papa!" with the bold impunity of a fearless toddler. Changing his diaper is often a physical act that requires two people, leaving us tired, sweaty, and mentally broken. When we are done, I often feel like I might need to change my diaper too. My son will be eighteen years old by 2032, and I wish him the best of luck, but I wish he were more interested in judo or table tennis.

Even my daughter, who has now graduated to a toilet, will not free me from her potty grasp. She'll often sit there for many minutes doing her deed—and she prefers to have company. It gets lonely in there on that big toilet, she tells me. Together, she and I sit in the bathroom, talking about deep things or reading a book together as she grunts it all out with a cherry-red face. "Done, Papa!"

By the nature of my profession, I cannot hope to escape this poop experience at work either. It is such a prominent part of the day of a pediatric nurse that we can't even be grossed out by it anymore. The poop I witness, test, flush, and handle often passes right through yuck territory all the way through to hilarious land.

In the hospital, we typically describe urgent situations as a code corresponding with a particular color. Code White indicates a pediatric medical emergency—come help now. Code Red, a fire emergency—remove, extinguish, and contain. We even have a code to indicate an active shooter, which would be Code Silver—hide or run away. And, unofficially of course, there is the infamous Code Brown that indicates the presence of a poop emergency, a time when the poop is simply out of control—enter at your own risk. If you do come in, wear gloves.

I remember one day back in nursing school when a nurse tapped me on the shoulder as she ran down the hall on some other urgent business. Before she disappeared into a patient's room, she asked me to help her other patient, a Ms. Hong in Room 9, to the bathroom.

Because I was a student who wished to be helpful, I accepted what would surely be an easy task and made my way to the room. I fully expected to expertly and kindly escort the frail and elderly Ms. Hong to the bathroom or commode, let her do her business, and then gently get her back in bed. Easy peasy. I had yet to experience a true poop emergency in my short time in the hospital, and my kids would not poop in this world for yet another ten years to come.

I was surprised to learn that "helping Ms. Hong get to the bathroom" was actually a euphemism for a Code Brown that the nurse was trying to avoid. The scene I walked into in Room 9 was a flushed and elderly Ms. Hong standing in the middle of what was easily a three-foot-wide puddle of diarrhea. The distressed old woman was yelling and waving her arms in a pleading, chicken-like manner. I did not need to speak Mandarin to understand what she was saying: HELP ME.

So, I put on some gloves. Then, I put some more gloves on over the first pair and did the best I could. It went okay. Ms. Hong made it to the bathroom where she surprisingly continued to defecate even more—an act that seemed inconceivable based on her prior output. With the help of another nursing student, I cleaned her up and got her back to bed. It was not what I would have chosen to do, but it felt good to help another person.

Kirsten once told me the story of her personal all-time favorite Code Brown. She was in a room with another nurse, caring for a teenage girl who was experiencing "massively explosive diarrhea all over the room." It was all over the floor, all over the bed, and all over the patient—shit almost permeated their innermost souls.

"It was everywhere," Kirsten recounted, "and we were stuck in the room until we could have the floors mopped, or at least until we could clean the bottoms of our shoes." Kirsten happened to be the charge nurse that evening, and although the rest of the floor was quite chaotic, full of patients and their nurses who needed her assistance, she could not leave this girl's room. Her phone was buzzing and vibrating with urgent messages and calls, but there was no way to escape her task without tracking diarrhea prints down the hall.

"We were trying to clean this girl up and she was yelling at us to hurry. My partner in this chaos was holding and bear-hugging this unruly patient as I was up in her business, wiping her ass and trying not to snicker," Kirsten snickered freely at the thought of that memory. Although the situation had been slightly intense, Kirsten's experience of it was not negative. She could still laugh about it without making that poor girl the butt of the joke—pun very much intended.

MOM AND DAD, TAKE CARE OF YOURSELVES

We had really good moments...if it wasn't for this cancer. That's what was hard about being in the hospital. You lose control of that. You don't have control of who comes into the room or what energy they bring—how much fear. I became sensitive to that.

– Susan, Ari's Mom

"Papa...wake up...keep reading, Papa," pleaded my daughter as I once again nodded off in her bed, a Roald Dahl book precariously tented over my nose. My son had resisted a daytime nap and as a result had already surrendered to sleep. He was draped across my chest like a human blanket. His soft snores beckoned me to join his slumber like mermaids singing to a land-starved sailor.

Every time I succumbed to the sirens, though, my daughter pulled me back to the land of the living. Even though every cell in my body was exhausted, she was not a bit tired. I tried to read the book once more, but inevitably the sentences reshuffled into a meaningless word salad as I drifted off once again.

It was not until I became a dad that I understood how truly draining parent life actually is. The aspects of my lifestyle that I had once taken for granted—peace and quiet, a steady and self-directed schedule, and a reliable good night's sleep—suddenly were no longer guaranteed. I now had to consider the well-being of my children and my partner along with my own needs.

My frail illusion was smashed to pieces a few days after we first brought our baby daughter home from the hospital. It was three in the morning, and her colicky screams echoed relentlessly between her mouth, my forehead, and the walls of our one-bedroom apartment. It was in that moment—trembling, half-awake, with my bedhead pointing in every direction—that I realized what we had done. We were parents now.

Even when we get the kids to bed at a reasonable hour, a late-night visit is inevitable. Deep into the night, at least one of my children will regularly scream out as if someone is amputating one of their feet. On one of the rare silent nights when we make it to morning undisturbed, my daughter wakes us up no later than 6 a.m., pleading for cereal, needing to poop, or simply for some company.

"It's your turn," says my half-awake wife. I do not respond, because I am either still sleeping or pretending to sleep. No forensic expert would be able to determine the difference.

Ironically though, I learned to appreciate the value of sleep long before I had children of my own. It is the dire, sleep-deprived situation experienced by so many of the parents I work with that taught me. These parents never signed up for the many uncomfortable nights they must spend in the hospital and all the mental anguish and fatigue that comes along with being a good parent to a sick child. It is their discomfort and universal fatigue that is a constant reminder to me of the importance of sleep and basic self-care for all parents.

Peace and quiet is an elusive amenity here. For our patients and their families who spend weeks, months, or even years in the hospital, access to uninterrupted sleep is a hard thing to come by. Finding alone time is also impossible. The most that families can reasonably expect is a polite and perfunctory warning knock from a near constant wave of hospital staff. My nurse colleagues have definitely walked into quite a few awkward situations in which parents of young, sleeping children were not expecting a visit. The details are perhaps best left to your colorful imagination, but the recollection of one of my nurse friends, "All I saw was a very pale body making it for the bathroom," completes the picture well. Even in the hospital, ovulation waits for no one.

The hospital can be a difficult place to recover from illness. The sheer amount of technology built into how we care for people in our current medical paradigm ensures a steady supply of beeps, blings, and critical blares all throughout the day and night. Even the patients' beds join the chorus of night noise, emitting a continuous groaning sound as air is slowly shifted within the mattress in order to prevent patients from developing pressure ulcers. Some patients find this subtle shifting surface to be soothing, but most find it to be incredibly annoying.

The ever-present and well-intentioned interruption of machines and their human helpers can take a very real toll on the well-being of both patients and parents. Long after her young daughter had been successfully treated for leukemia and they were all back home, Jeni, the mother of a cute toddler named Gertie, told me about her year of sleep deprivation in the hospital.

Due to the nature of her daughter's disease, Jeni and Gertie often remained in the hospital for months at a time. During the night, Jeni kept the TV on so it would blend in with the constant sounds of pumps and people. Even so, she woke up every time a nurse came into the room. She jumped to attention every time her daughter shifted in her crib. She was often delirious and highly emotional because of it.

Sleep is important for our parents. They are often expected to understand and consent to high-risk treatments. In many cases, especially with an acutely ill child, the course of this care may change daily. I cannot imagine staying on top of a complex treatment plan, attending to the needs of a sick child, and also managing basic care for myself while being severely sleep-deprived. At home with my two toddlers in the morning, semi-catatonic from the previous night, the biggest decision I usually have to make is between cereal and waffles. It still is not an easy one—not until I have had my coffee, at least.

Although the questions I ask myself each day as a father of healthy kids are vastly different than the ones the parents I work with face, they do at times overlap. These parents must encounter their own fears of the unknown and the many night-whispers that haunt their hearts and heads. These whispers may be more disturbing than the beeps of a machine or the accidental banging shuffle of a night nurse. These voices may ask unanswerable questions such as:

Have I made the right decisions?

Will my baby be the exception?

Have I done everything I can to save my child's life?

And, at times...

What will I do without my child?

As a parent of two healthy kids, who is all too aware of how lucky I am to be in this position, these are the burning questions that keep me up at night:

How long will it be before I feel like a good parent?

Will my kids survive emotionally intact while I get there?

How do I balance the needs of my wife and kids with my own needs?

And, finally...

What would I do if my own kids were seriously ill, or if they died?

Unfortunately, for all parents of kids both healthy and ill, there are no easy answers to any of these questions. We must navigate this uncertain terrain without a map and hope that we end up where we want to be and that the journey was interesting. Parenting isn't for the meek nor for those who depend on routine. There is no GPS, no machine to tell you which way to turn. You have to figure it out on your own, and sometimes, simply enjoy being lost.

Susan, Ari's mother, spoke to me candidly about how it felt to pass a night in the hospital. She is a palliative care nurse by profession. Even though she had made the art of caring for dying people her life's work, she too was subjected to the same uncertainty and unease that comes with being in the hospital with a sick child of your own. Her medical experience may have even been a liability. She knew exactly how deadly her dear son's disease was. Her fears plagued her the most during the night as her son Ari slept only a few feet away.

"You don't get much sleep in the hospital," she told me. "I think you change your expectations. I was happy if I could just go horizontal. If there was a problem, then everything was just amplified as far as being anxious. Things were just scarier in the middle of the night. Time and the atmosphere just became really surreal. I remember the difference when I would go out of the hospital and get some fresh air after being inside for a number of days. It was just really different...It was always wonderful leaving the hospital because the hospital was always full of fear. Coming home always felt safe and relaxed. In the hospital, you are there because there is a problem, and everything they are talking about is worrisome."

Susan described to me the mind exercises she often practiced in order to help manage runaway thoughts that frightened her at night. In order to tamp down this fear, she focused and paid attention to her body and named what the fear felt like. It felt "cold and like a pit in my stomach," she told me. There was no way to ignore this fear, so identifying it and diving into it helped her understand it for what it truly was.

Most nurses are accustomed to a similar state of exhaustion. The job of caring for acutely sick children deep into the night is taxing and grueling. Those of us who have done it can speak to that queasy, zombie-inducing four a.m. hour when the journey to change-of-shift at seven a.m. feels like staring across the Grand Canyon and wondering how you are possibly going to make it to the other side. Because we have an intimate understanding of exhaustion, we do our best to provide a calm and nurturing environment for our patients when possible.

Unfortunately, our many necessary medical interventions at all hours of the day and night threaten this peace. At this point in my career I work very few night shifts, but when I was a younger, I did so often. It is difficult to stay completely silent when entering a patient's room at night. I commonly found myself holding my breath for longer than was probably healthy and exiting the room a bit sweaty and tired from the exertion. As I would stand outside the door, my work done for a moment, I would express a sigh of relief that I had not dropped or knocked anything, waking up everyone in the room.

I have not always been so lucky. During one early morning blood draw, I accidentally bumped a metal lab tray, causing it to crash to the floor. The resulting gong-like clang frightened my patient and his parents out of a deep sleep.

Kirsten, a nurse who once worked almost exclusively during the night shift, confided in me about the challenges she saw. She lamented that "the hardest part about being a night nurse is when you come across families who always want it to be pitch black in their room. They don't want you to wake up their kid. They don't want you to touch their kid. That is really stressful because you can't do your job in the dark. You can't be quiet all the time. You have to be able to touch the patient. What happens if I can't see if they are breathing? It is not always safe doing what we have to do at night."

Nurses must balance providing the best possible care with maintaining some semblance of tranquility for patients and their families. Many of our night nurses like to think of themselves as veritable nurse ninjas who are able to enter and exit a patient's room without making a sound in those dark spaces. These nurses possess a unique skill of muscle memory, finesse, and patience that is often developed only after a great deal of experience working in the dark. This art form provides nocturnal caregivers a great deal of work satisfaction.

Jess, one of our most senior night staff, told me with no shortage of pride, "I love when a family can say, 'God, I got such great sleep last night. I didn't hear you at all,' when I had been in their room all night. I love for my families to get rest because it is so important for them to be on point during the day."

Jess, whose healing and personal talents are many, is also a skilled baby whisperer. She told me about the thoughtful way in which she approaches babies when she must check their vital signs very late in the night. "I always whisper to the babies before I touch them...They hear you before you turn the knob. I lean down and whisper to them...Even with the littlest babies, if you talk to them, it makes them aware that you are there. You don't go and grab at these kids...The only thing that these families are in control of is what is happening in that room at that time. They have no control of what is happening in their lives, so you just have to be respectful of their space. I enter every single patient room as if I am entering someone's house."

For a time, we do our best to make it a home—a home you can sleep in.

REMEMBER WHAT YOU HAVE

When you are very present and when you just slow down, almost anything feels intimate—especially with a dying patient.

- Amy, pediatric oncology nurse, mother

When a child dies in our care, we bathe their body. This is an act of reverence, a way for us all to remember and say goodbye. It is a cleansing ritual, often motivated by our close relationship to that child, but we do it still even if we did not know the patient well when they were living.

A few years into my career, I had taken care of many children who were close to the end of their lives. By sheer chance, none of these patients had passed away while I was their nurse. There were days—as I cared for unconscious children whose breathing had slowed to a crawl—when I was quite sure it would happen. By the end of those long shifts though, these children still held onto their lives and I went home to live mine.

The first child I helped to bathe was not one who I had known well before he died. The boy's parents had already left by the time I entered the room, yet the space did not feel abandoned. The bright morning sun inhabited the room like a watchful sentinel, its soft light rendering every object more blanched and neutral.

This was especially true of the dead boy in the bed. He was naked except for his diaper, his smooth skin almost as pale as the pristine white sheet he was on. Some dark-blue sheets had been inscrutably placed next to his bed. I was later told that these thick drapes are used to hide pools of blood should a dying patient bleed out at the end. They remained unused that day.

As another nurse and I bathed the boy, we said very little—hushed words within short sentences—just enough to coordinate our actions. Except for the gentle slosh of washcloths being dipped into the warm, sudsy water, the room was quiet. I remember that he was a slight boy—not more than forty pounds—but inert as he was, he felt much heavier. I held his little, limp hand in mine and lifted his arm as another nurse gently scrubbed underneath. My blue glove contrasted sharply with his light, almost translucent skin.

I had been nervous about what the experience of bathing a deceased child would be like, apprehensive about how it would feel to touch the skin of a dead person: the coldness, the weight, death so palpable in my hands. What I have learned is that when you wash the body of the dead, they don't help you. They do not respond to a gentle tug. The playful roll-over command is lost into the ether. They don't fight you either. There is no splashing or wriggling. Nothing. You do everything for them. This act is surprisingly challenging and usually requires two nurses—one to hold and one to wash. For a short time, we become a child's motor. We move them and we make them clean.

Many parents choose not to bathe the body of their deceased child and I understand why: the act of bathing their dead child is yet another torturous experience, among many that have already occurred and all those that will surely come. It is not therapy for them, just more pain.

For others though, this difficult act is a necessary part of the healing process. I remember one mom who asked for water to be heated up so she could wash her teenage daughter shortly after she had passed. It had been a truly traumatic and painful death for this girl and her family. Just moments before, this mother had been lying on top of her daughter's body, screaming in misery.

When the girl's nurse brought the warm water to the bedside though, the mom was calm. She delicately dipped the back of her hand into the small plastic tub, checking the temperature. It was not right for her daughter, she decided.

"Could you please warm it up more?" she asked her nurse kindly. She then lovingly cleaned her daughter's body. She washed her hair, blew it dry, and carefully styled it. Before her nurses brought the girl's body down to the morgue, her mother gave her a manicure.

For those parents who choose to take part in it, I think this bath represents the last moment in which they may serve one who is dear to them. It is the final time they will physically commune with them too, touch them. They may not have been able to cleanse their child of their disease or the pain and anguish which it brought, but they can clean their child's body once their pain is over. They can wash away the dirt of a world that offered no reprieve and little kindness.

Although often powerless to prevent the death of our children, we can control how we interact with them when they are alive, and for a short time after they have died. I understand the compulsion to want to keep that control for as long as possible, to be useful in any way.

For me, the most important and fulfilling part of parenthood is being useful to my children. I cannot imagine having to let go of them sooner than expected. I would choose to hold on as well, even if just for one more bath.

When it has been my duty to care for a child in this way, I have tried to do so with the heart of a father—even before I actually was one. In all these interactions I have with these children lying before me, dead or still living, I treat them like they were my own. I learned how to do this—how to be this way—by following the example of the same nurse mentors who instructed me in the care of these patients as they lived. It was a lesson mostly without words.

When we bathe these children, we are gentle and kind. There is no hurry or haste. We may softly sing songs that we know they liked and once sang along with us. If they still have the hair on their heads, we brush it until it appears as they once preferred it to be. As we clean their limbs, torso, and face, we sometimes laugh or smile as we remember funny things they said or did. We talk to these kids too—like we would have when they were still alive—and we are content when they do not reply as they once might have.

"I'm going to clean your face now, sweetie," I remember saying once to a child who could not possibly answer back.

Even while engaged in such care at the hospital, I don't stop being a dad. When I leave for home, I don't magically cease being a nurse. These two roles have somehow joined together to form the imperfect whole that is me. Perhaps that is who Nurse Papa truly is—a caregiver who feels most at home in a place that exists perpetually in between. Although the synergy can be disorienting, it also feels completely natural.

At the end of a day like this, I return home and, along with my wife, bathe our own children, read them stories, and put them to bed. It is a ritual that is equal parts utilitarian tumult and pure, floating fun. It is a raucous, giggly, occasionally tearful, definitely more water on the bathroom floor than in the tub, shampoo-mohawk filled affair. As my kids flip and flounder in the too-small tub, their wonderfully healthy and intact bodies splashing each other and splashing me, I sometimes lack the necessary parental stamina and patience to make it all the way from wet and soapy to dry with pajamas on.

"STOP SPLASHING YOUR BROTHER!" I order my daughter. The small, echoey space of the bathroom makes my command sound much louder and rougher than I intended it to be. It doesn't seem to matter though. She ignores me.

Her younger brother, who was red-eyed and crying just moments earlier, is giggling now too, splashing back. My kids are nudists by nature, and this bath time—this wet, naked chaos—is their happy place. No matter how soaked or pissed off I may be, it is my happy place too.

As I dry off my son's plump, cherubic body, I marvel at how healthy and strong he feels in my arms. Still holding him, I regard the wet footprints tracked down the hall by the sylph-like girl who just rejected my towel. She is no longer in sight, but I can hear her causing wet trouble in another part of our house. As my irritation subsides, I realize what I have. Tonight, my kids are with me. Tonight, they are clean.

DAVID METZGER, R.N.

BREAK FROM THE HEARTBREAK
SILLY WILL SAVE YOU

If we didn't laugh at ourselves, or the shitty situations we sometimes find ourselves in, I don't think we would be able to cope very well with what we do. For me, to be able to laugh at work is one of the best parts of our job.

- Kirsten, pediatric oncology nurse

It is the people I spend time with in the hospital who so often make my job such a fun and gratifying experience. With my nurse friends—people with whom I have shared so many traumatic and dark times—I have learned to smile and laugh even when we are sad together. It is a unique bond we share. Our ability to be silly in the most inappropriate moments helps us to return the next day for more of those hard moments, knowing we will be supported, loved, and understood. The children I care for and the parents who care for them are also a hopeful inspiration to me. The wisest of them have learned, through trial and heartache, that laughter is often the best medicine. It is incorruptible to despair even in the most desperate of times.

One of the funniest lines I ever heard in my life came from the deadpan mouth of a mother standing over her dying teenage daughter. I had just walked into the girl's hospital room to help Danielle, her nurse that day. Danielle has bright-blue eyes, a naughty smile, and a quirky sense of humor, but none of these qualities prepared her for what she heard next. She was concentrating on the medication pump next to her patient's bed in order to give the girl an extra dose of morphine.

In that moment, the girl's mother remarked in my direction: "Oh, I see you have a woody, and poo on your shirt too." She was referring to the two patches I had sewn to my nurse's scrubs: A classic Winnie-the-Pooh holding a honey pot and Woody from Toy Story peeking out of my right pocket, but Danielle did not know that. She whipped her head around in my direction, fully expecting the worst from this young male nurse until she too was in on the joke. It was an unexpected quip from a mom who certainly had nothing to laugh about in that moment, but there she was anyway, making a perfectly on-point joke.

In that hilarious moment, I was too busy examining my scrub top for shit stains and my pants for an undesired hard-on to fully share in the laugh. Years later, after I became fully initiated to the trials and tribulations of parenthood, I could appreciate that mother's joke for what it truly was: a Hail Mary, a lifeline, a desperate attempt to dispel any small part of the misery she must have been experiencing. And it seemed to work for her—at least for a short time—and that was good enough.

With my own two children, who seem uniquely manufactured to decimate my patience on an hourly basis, I am often unable to find the humor in life or even control my temper. There are moments, though, when I somehow break through the feelings of anger and frustration that are routine to raising kids both sick and healthy. I find myself in an entirely new place in which my emotional discomfort still exists, but no longer has the same power over me. When I am able to summon this state, I am a much better father. I'm also able to find joy in the hard times when they invariably show up because I feel like I am in on the joke, rather than the cosmic butt of it.

DON'T FEEL LIKE YOU HAVE TO FIX EVERYTHING

He died happy. He may have been in pain. He may have been suffering, but he died happy. That is what is important.

- Jeff, hospital pastor, father

With my two kids, I often feel challenged to make everything alright. The goal is impossible; I can't fix everything, but I can fix some things. In the hospital with my young patients, this is also true. I am often helpless to save a life or stop the pain, but this does not mean that I am completely powerless.

When Jason first came to us, he was broken and close to death. From the perspective of the nursing and medical team, there was little pretense of a cure or significant life extension. I can't say if this reality was fully understood by Jason or his family, but such acceptance often lags behind the knowing experience of caregivers who have seen it many times before.

Jason had been expecting to receive a new liver to replace his failing one. Before this could happen, his surgeons discovered a giant tumor. It was wrapped around Jason's liver and intestines like an octopus clinging to a coral reef. It was inoperable. This, of course, made Jason ineligible for the expected transplant. The tumor would kill him before his dysfunctional liver would.

Meeting Jason for the first time was like walking into a cinematic memory. He was a teenager, but his appearance reminded me of the extraterrestrial from the movie E.T. His body was a study in contrasts. His torso was so cachectic from poor nutrition that his ribs pushed against his skin like steps leading up to a hugely distended belly. His arms and legs were long and lanky like those of an awkward adolescent, but atrophic and knobby at the joints like those typically found on an old man. When he tried to stand up, his body swayed side to side and his limbs wobbled like bamboo stalks in the wind.

Jason's skin was pale yellow and marked by bruises on his arms where peripheral IVs had been placed, lost, and placed again. His hair, ruffled and unkempt, was reddish brown. It stood on top of a pale and slightly pocked face that was dominated by thick eyeglasses resting upon a sharp and narrow nose. He often squinted myopically through the lenses at his slender fingered hands, contemplating his fingernails, which were unexpectedly long.

At times, Jason's room seemed more like a setting for a family reunion than a hospital room. There was a rotating cast of aunts and uncles milling about above a troop of young, cow-licked cousins playing among themselves on the floor. I sometimes needed to strategically weave through a few relatives to get to Jason.

Despite the noisy chaos of his family, Jason did not interact much except to occasionally ask for something he needed or to whisper some soft, secret words in his dad's ear. When the effort of speech was too much for him, he would slowly raise a shaky arm, tethered by IV lines. It was a gesture meant to silence the room enough to allow him an audience. His family, loud and boisterous, quickly hushed as we all awaited direction to assist him. More often than not, Jason's hand returned to earth with no clear message delivered other than his obvious frustration.

When Jason first spoke directly to me, I couldn't make out his words. His muffled voice came out in a nearly indiscernible whisper from a set of pale, chapped lips, as if some invisible hand was pulling the words back down his throat. In order to understand what he was saying, I had to place my ear very close to his face. In this very intimate position, I could feel his irregular breaths on my cheek and see his heart beating softly on the surface of his chest.

"Where's my dad?" he asked again after clearing his throat, and this time I understood him.

Jason's dad—a small man with buzzed hair and a receding hairline—had sad, squinty eyes that did not match the ever-present grin on his face. He had stepped out to get something from the nearby van he had been sleeping in.

Normally, though, he was a fixture in Jason's room. He was constantly joking around with his son, affectionately touching him, and engaging with him in a goofy way. Although his encouraging quips were often strange and slightly inappropriate, he seemed to be the perfect antidote to the sometimes impenetrably somber situation Jason found himself in.

At one point, Jason's dad admitted to me with a secretive smirk that he had been circumspectly supplying his son with medical marijuana suppositories to help ease his discomfort. "I'll do whatever I have to do to make him feel better," he told me.

Before having children of my own, I wondered how these sick children could face their circumstances in a way that was positive and heartening rather than just depressing. How did their parents support and nurture a process that's end was often the death of their child? Jason's dad and many parents like him have shown me that there is a way to reframe the pain by accepting it and finding the joy that exists in living while also dying.

I have marveled at how one particular mother I worked with engaged with her sick boy in a physical and playful way. Instead of reacting to her own fears and his stress, she showed him an entirely different path.

Whenever her son began to cry or scream out of fear, she drew his thin body close to hers. With her face pressed lightly against his cheek, she whispered sweet words into his ear. She pulled playfully at his toes, each of which had a name, until he was once again giggling and smiling. Most likely, she was quieting her own inner turmoil too. Although he eventually passed away, the life he lived in those last few months seemed somehow so full and meaningful. It was his mother who made that possible.

I learned to use a very similar tactic of redirection with my own kids at home. When my daughter is intractably upset and writhing on the floor because I will not give her what she wants, I try to get right down on the floor with her and provide the very thing she needs—my love, my attention, and my presence. I gently tickle her ribs or her tiny feet until she can no longer suppress the giggles she is trying so hard to hold back. If more is required, I nuzzle a piggishly snorting nose upon her neck and pretend to feast on her chin until she is laughing and has forgotten that she was ever sad.

This silly connection also helps me forget how annoyed I just was. It resets us both. Without altering the circumstances that were causing her pain, I helped change how she relates to it. These are the moments when I am the most successful in my role as a parent. The times when I fail miserably are when I question her existential pain altogether, when I disregard it rather than nurture and reframe it.

As his days in our care passed into weeks, even Jason's father was unable to comfort his son. Jason's intense, physical agony would often break through the strong medications he was receiving. Nothing was working to cool the fire within him and, lacking any other resource, Jason just began to shut down, to fully retreat within himself.

In a way, Jason's pain became his whole identity, the only face he presented to the world around him. It was difficult to know anything about him beyond the physical torment that dominated his daily existence. Just as he had no foreseeable future, it seemed to me, illogically, that he had no past as well—that he had always suffered like this. He was a body in pain, waiting to die.

Even though Jason was not the first patient I had seen suffering before death, the experience touched me in a new and uncomfortable way. My son, still incubating in his mom's womb, was to be born a few weeks into the future. In my mind, I could not reconcile the hopeful anticipation I felt for the arrival of my new child with the grotesque pain that was Jason's, as he prepared to leave that same world. I desperately wanted to change it, to make it alright, but it was not. That reality left me feeling impotent and useless. I thought that I was powerless to help this boy, but I was wrong. Although they influence each other, physical pain is different than existential pain. I stumbled upon a way to help Jason relate differently to his emotional distress, even though I could do little to soothe the distress in his body.

Jason had not allowed us to bathe him in many days—even the most modest exertion left him dazed and sapped of energy. Also, I imagine that something as mundane as a bath must seem so trivial when you are young and dying. After some gentle coaxing, and mostly so I would finally leave him alone, Jason agreed to let me wash him. He was so weak that it required three of us to do the job in a way that he could physically bear.

Like dance partners in some sad waltz, Jason and I stood facing each other, his arms draped limply over my shoulders. He was fully naked. I held him firmly under his arms as my colleagues bathed him: scrubbing his boney back, shampooing his stringy and mussed hair. The side of Jason's face lightly touched mine as we stood there, and again, I could hear him breathing sharp, clipped inhalations. Though we washed him quite gently, it was clear that the experience was very uncomfortable. When one of us touched him in the wrong way, his long fingernails pressed firmly into my skin. It felt as if his hands were trying to claw their way out of a deep hole. He was shivering and shaking.

When we were finally done, though, Jason glowed like a brand-new boy. His skin was scrubbed and sweet smelling. His damp hair was now neatly parted to one side. As he lay back on a freshly made bed, he clasped both of his hands gently behind his neck in a state of gentle repose.

I smiled at him. Regarding me through his thick eyeglasses, he seemed to actually see me for the first time, and a faint smile, which I had never seen before, rested on his pale face. He shifted his gaze to the ceiling and took in a deep, cleansing breath. In that moment, Jason looked more like a relaxed sunbather on a balmy beach than a dying boy in a hospital bed.

While bathing Jason, it had not been my intention to do much more than clean his body. I was not trying to fix him. I knew that was not possible. In the five short minutes it took us to bathe him, I was completely present with Jason. I saw him in a whole new way, and I believe he saw me from an altered vantage too. Similar to my perfectly healthy children at home who often feel that their entire world is tumbling down, the understanding presence of a caring human was what Jason needed then. It did not fix him, but I think it fed his soul.

Later that day, it was just him and me, alone in his room—a rare moment when his loving yet somewhat dysfunctional family had stepped out for their own self-care: cannabis, cigarettes, and cafeteria food (or some combination thereof). A late-summer afternoon sun tried in vain to invade the room with its soft orange light, but it was foiled by the heavy shades on the windows. The room felt womb-like—a cave for two people. It was so quiet I could hear the soft motor of the IV pump delivering its medication to its target—this boy. Jason was still basking in the glow of his bath and I had thought he was sleeping when he suddenly spoke to me.

"David, do you have any pets at home?" he asked in a rough but resolute whisper that cut like a scalpel through the silence of the room. I was surprised when he used my first name.

"Yes," I answered, "we have a cat, but she gets mostly ignored these days because we have a baby girl too."

"We have cats too, three of them," he said, "but we had to put one of them down. She was old and she wouldn't eat."

"It's sad when that happens to someone you love," I told him.

"Yeah, it is," he responded, "but it is something you have to get used to if you love cats."

I had never heard Jason put together so many words out loud, much less words that were so self-reflective and metaphorical. I can only believe that the calm and intimate moments we had experienced that afternoon had helped him find those words to share with me.

It is something you have to get used to if you love cats. Those words echoed in my mind again and again as I and many others cared for Jason over the next couple of weeks.

Then, as we all expected he would, he died. Mikko, the nurse who was taking care of Jason the night he passed away, instinctively placed her hand on the head of Jason's dad as he knelt crying beside his son. As she comforted this grieving father, tears streamed silently down her cheeks too.

WHEN TO EMBRACE YOUR EMOTIONS

I can't ever manage my tears in my personal life, but at work it is often necessary. For me to be able to function and do things I need to do, I can't cry.

- Cassi, pediatric oncology nurse, mother

For me, one of the most challenging aspects of being a dad is knowing when to fully engage and, of course, when not to. Very often, I realize that I have way too much emotional skin in the game to act or react reasonably with my children. I have to step away. With the kids in the hospital too, understanding when to lay my heart bare requires an emotional honesty that, still to this day, I am working on. These young patients teach me how to be a good parent as well as a decent human, just as my own children do.

Armen was once an active and energetic teenager. One day though, while descending the stairs of the school bus, he fell to the ground. He did not know it at the time, but there was a tumor growing out of control within his brain and his spine. It had overtaken the nerves that communicated from his brain to the rest of his body, causing him to lose control of his legs. He could move his arms only with great effort, but he could no longer control his body below his chest. That casual descent from the school bus—an act that he had performed thousands of times before—marked the end of his innocence and the beginning of a new, much heavier reality.

Armen's father, who shared a name with his son, was there

the day Armen was transferred to our oncology floor on a gurney.
Armen, the father, was in his mid-forties, but his thinning grey hair
and gaunt cheeks suggested that he was much older. I thought to
myself that he had either led a very hard life or, perhaps more likely,
he had aged ten years in the past ten weeks. He had an easy smile,
though, and his accented voice was pleasant and surprisingly high-
pitched. He seemed relieved that he and Armen would no longer
be subjected to the close medical scrutiny of the pediatric intensive
care unit—a place where patient rooms have no doors, just sliding
glass walls.

I was happy to meet them both, but I was concerned for
them too. Although I shared their relief at Armen's move from the
critical care unit, this was just the beginning of a long journey for this
boy and his family. The disease Armen suffered from is called an
atypical teratoid rhabdoid tumor, or ATRT. It is exceedingly rare,
and the cure rate is quite low. Until that day, I had not seen it afflict
a child older than two years old, and rarely had I seen it as advanced
as it was in Armen.

At best, I thought to myself, this boy might regain some
of the bodily functions that he had lost, but he will likely not
survive beyond a year. I did not say this of course, but I could not
control my awareness of it. We nurses come to this place to care
for sick children and cannot afford to be naive to all the morbid
possibilities. This sad understanding is an emotional tightrope that
most experienced nurses must walk across. We must balance our
clinical awareness of the odds and our inner desire for the patients
we love to somehow be the lucky outliers.

At first, as Armen and his dad settled into their new
surroundings, we just chatted and got to know each other. Armen
was looking around with a neutral expression. He was taking in his

new, sunny room and the smiling nurse in blue standing before him. His flat look indicated that he had not yet made up his mind about either. In order to make him feel more comfortable, I asked him about specific ways he preferred his care to be carried out—should I ask before I touched him? What did he like to be called? Armen told me that he preferred that I call him Sheroz, the name given to him by his father. In his language it means King of Roses.

Later on, Armen admitted that he had been confused by my questions at first. Nobody in the hospital he had come from had ever asked him what he thought. The medical institution he had transferred from had misdiagnosed his disease and mismanaged his care for months.

Due to the neurological damage caused by his tumor, one half of Armen's face was stuck in a perpetual droop, but I learned to tell when he was smiling. The curve of his lips on the right side of his face would turn slightly upward. Below an endearing unibrow, Armen's boyish cheeks were blemished with a spray of teenage acne and the faint sprouts of what would one day be dark facial hair. He was an adolescent with one foot firmly placed in boyhood while the other poked gingerly into the realm of young adulthood. Neither of these feet would move under his own power again.

That day, Armen's dad asked me about the colorful wristbands that, over my nearly ten years as a nurse, I had accumulated around the neck of my stethoscope. I had copied this habit from one of my favorite doctors on the floor. I told the Armens that these bands, imprinted with declarations of hope and the names of children, were given to me by just a few of the many young patients I had taken care of over the years.

The suggestion that I had known many other kids who had undergone a similar strife as Armen seemed to make them both happy. "He's taken care of so many children, Armen," said his dad. Armen did not respond, but the right side of his lips turned almost imperceptibly to the ceiling. It was the first time I saw him smile.

More often than not, a child's march toward death is slow and strangely predictable. It is a process of incremental diminution, a silent and pernicious theft of autonomy and personality. This journey often takes a long time. In many ways, this time is a gift to their caretakers, not only because their lives are extended, but because we truly get the opportunity to know these children and their parents. These children are able to be with their loved ones and choose, in their own personal way, how they want the rest of their life to look.

It is impossible not to get emotionally involved. I get close to some of these kids in ways that, still today, feels unexpected. Over the course of caring for a sick child, from diagnosis to death, I often learn what's going on in their lives—the silly dramas, their likes and dislikes, their fears and dreams, all the way down to the name of their uncle's girlfriend's dog. At times, these lives become emotionally entwined with mine in a way that does not always end when I leave work to be with my own family.

In a way, I take these kids home with me. As I put my own children to bed, I sometimes say good night to the children in the hospital too. I silently hope that their nights go well—that their conditions remain stable, that they don't get scared, that their parents manage to get some much-needed sleep.

This intimacy between child and caregiver also stems from the utilitarian necessities of the job of a nurse. In my daily physical assessment of these children, I must listen closely to the sounds of their bodies—their lungs, their hearts, and their bowels. These secret noises become as familiar to me as their voices, their laughs, and their cries do.

As I assess these vital organs through my stethoscope, their owners very rarely remain quiet or still. The squeaks and rhythms often combine with bits of conversation, random giggles, and excited exclamations. I don't know my own children in this way. When I play doctor/patient with my daughter, the sick one is usually a Barbie doll dressed like a mermaid. Rarely do I examine my kids from head to toe like I do my young patients.

Due to the extreme circumstances that we navigate in the hospital, we form profound relationships quickly. One nurse I spoke to, Amy, told me how over the course of a shift and for a brief moment in time, she entered that most intimate space with a dying patient and his family—a group of people she had never before encountered.

"I didn't have a relationship with this family," she recalled with a wistful smile on her face, her deep-blue eyes focusing on something in the distance. "The kid was dying, and he had come to us because he was afraid to die at home. I was nervous because he clearly was going to die on my shift, but I met the family and they were quite lovely. They were sharing stories about this young man and letting me know about him...He ended up passing that day, and I bathed him after he died. His parents had told me that he loved jazz music and that he was a musician, so when we did his last bath, we put on jazz music...You want to respect this person like they are someone you have loved all your life. We played beautiful music for him."

Armen would become one of those children with whom I formed a close bond. I felt deeply for this boy from the moment we met. In him, I saw a young man whose interior world was complex and so very sad. He reminded me a bit of myself when I was his age.

And, like two souls left together on a deserted island, our

closeness was not always a choice, but rather a consequence of how much time we spent together. I am one of only a small group of male nurses on my floor. Armen preferred that it be one of us who took care of him. Having a male nurse put him at ease. If that male could also have a relaxed humor and bring some levity to the room, even better.

Armen was not always easy to be around. He could be sweet and thoughtful, but there were also times when his lack of physical progress and utter boredom in the hospital made him distant and cold. During these moments, even my attempts at humor fell flat and Armen scolded me for making light of his feelings. In turn, I would ask for his forgiveness, just as I do with my own kids when I fail to fully comprehend their interior lives or make light of something important to them. I allowed him to see my imperfections in a way that made me vulnerable. It was a conscious choice to do so. I loved him.

Caring for Armen was demanding in other ways too. Over the course of a shift, Armen's nurse had to assist him in almost every single personal activity—shifting and cleaning his body, eating and drinking, and even urinating.

Four or five times a shift, I needed to insert a catheter into Armen's urethra in order to help him safely empty his bladder. To do it correctly, I stood over Armen for up to fifteen minutes at a time—one hand holding the catheter that I had carefully inserted and the other pushing gently on his bladder to further his peeing progress. This might seem awkward, but it rarely was. When he was in a good mood, Armen had a relaxed ease about him that allowed others to care for him without being embarrassed about it.

During those intimate sessions, Armen and I often chatted or joked around. He told me about his plans to walk again. To be a normal kid. It was a hope he held on to. He also told me about the things that most scared him. He was not scared of dying young because he never even considered it a possibility. What he feared most was that the kids at school might make fun of his radiation-induced baldness. Before I had a chance to reassure him, he said with a cute confidence that made me smile, "I'll just wear a hat, David. Then, they won't even notice that my hair is gone."

"Don't worry if you can't find a hat," I joked. "You have a very symmetrical head, my friend."

One time, as we both contemplated the impossibly slow drip of his pee into the urinal, Armen asked me about my own family. For a moment—and I have no idea why—I got lost in the telling of a special time I had shared with my grandfather before he passed away. When I finished the story, Armen said, "David, you are crying."

After a surprised pause, I said, "I'm not crying, you goofball."

Armen countered, "Not from your eyes, no, but your heart is crying, David. I can hear it."

Armen was right. My heart had been crying, and I was not even aware of it until he had pointed it out. This boy's acute awareness of my subtle emotional cues left me speechless.

In most situations, nurses have a way of finding balance, but this process is not predictable. Corianna, who has always cared too much, told me about an exchange she once had with the mother of a dying girl. This woman shared her often intense and unfiltered feelings freely with the nurses who cared for and had great affection for her daughter.

"Why don't you cry when you come into the room?" the girl's mother asked Corianna as she knelt beside her patient. It was a strangely personal question to ask someone, but I understand why this mom asked it. Her daughter was all she could focus on. Distracted in her grief, she had no concept that the nurses would often need to protect their own emotions in order to come back every day and do their job.

"It's not that I am not sad," Corianna replied in a voice that I imagine as one long sigh, her large green eyes showing how badly she felt, "but I can't take good care of Casey and also take care of you if I am an emotional mess."

A strong emotional connection may serve to focus a nurse's attention on their patient in a way that is positive, but there is a chance it may do more harm than good. As a parent, I suffer from this phenomenon as well. My kids hurt my feelings constantly without ever knowing it. They challenge me with their antics and, at times, make me feel like a complete asshole. I am often unable to find the humor in it or even control my temper. When they reject me for their mother, or point out a simple truth that wounds my fragile ego, I feel it deeply, but I know I can't react to it every time it happens. To do so would scare them and it would not be an effective way to parent. Sometimes, I have to take a step back from my feelings as a human in order to be the best dad for these little humans.

As my kids get older and their internal worlds become more complex, I often feel less sure about how I will function as their dad in any given situation. The emotional map we all navigate together expands and changes. In order to survive the daily indignity of parenthood and raise halfway-decent kids, it feels necessary and healthy to sometimes compartmentalize my emotions from my parenting decisions, to not bother using the map at all.

As the day approached when Armen would leave our care, he was no closer to walking than when he first came to us. If anything, he was farther away from it. His body was weak and withered from months of inactivity. Although he would not admit it, his long silences and worried expressions indicated that he knew he would never be a normal boy again.

I was sad that I would not be seeing Armen anymore, but another part of me welcomed the change and the freedom away from the emotional exertion that, for me at least, his care entailed. To spend so much intimate time with him was as much a burden as it was a joy. With Armen, a boy I had grown so close to, I had to be a nurse first. I had to wall off my fondness for him in order to move on, too.

Many months later, Armen returned to our hospital to receive additional treatment. His growing tumor had weakened him further and had begun to affect his basic mental processing. Armen was often confused. His short-term memory was spotty, and his mood was more unpredictable. His dad—a person whom I had spent so much time with—had deteriorated in his own way as well. He seemed listless to me, like a broken and tired old man. His hair was whiter and thinner than it had been only months before.

When I encountered him in the hallway one day, I reflexively moved past the outstretched hand he first offered me and hugged him instead. Before we parted, he asked me to visit his son in his room when I could. I promised him I would. It was a normal and very simple request, but I didn't do it.

Over the next couple of weeks when they were still in the hospital, Armen and his dad passed on this same desire to other caregivers—that I stop by to visit—but still, I couldn't bring myself to see him. I did not pass by his room if I could avoid doing so. I was not assigned to take care of Armen over that time and, because he never left his room, it was easy to not see him.

Even so, the sad face of his father, Armen the elder, haunted me. In his tired stare, I saw and felt the pain of a parent rendered helpless and unable to protect his child. His sorrow reminded me of my own limitations as a dad and my own unspoken fears that it could all be taken from me without warning and for no good reason.

It is difficult to admit, but I did not visit Armen because I needed to protect myself. I could not witness his pain any longer. As we had gotten to know each other so well, it had felt right to absorb and be part of this boy's experience.

I was in a different place now. Armen's pain was no longer an emotional weight I chose to carry with me. I had built up a wall to block that pain. The map I previously used to navigate my feelings no longer existed. I had stepped off that road. I went home.

BREAK FROM THE HEARTBREAK
Funny Ha Ha

Ninjas do not like unicorns. Ninjas DO NOT take pictures with unicorns.

– Three-year-old oncology patient/ninja

For the most part, I have grown used to the extreme temperament changes that exist between the different patient rooms I must leave and re-enter many times over the course of a day. It is often the case that among my pediatric patients on any given day, some are very sick and sad while others are doing just fine and may even be preparing to go home.

On one day, just as I left a very sad room, the phone in my pocket alerted me to the needs of my other young patient that day, an eight-year-old named Kaspar. I could not quite hear what Kaspar was requesting—the speakerphone he was talking to me through had a sound quality similar to what you'd expect at a fast food drive-thru, minus the french fries.

Kaspar rarely intended to make me laugh, but he seldom failed to do so. His incredibly long isolation in the hospital at such an important developmental age often made him act strangely toward the caregivers who entered his room. He often could not be bothered to respond verbally when I tried to engage with him, but when he did, his answer often consisted of one interesting word.

"Good morning, Kaspar," I greeted him as I entered the room.

He was lost in the video game in front of him, but he did look

124

up for a brief moment and, with a blank expression, responded, "Penis."

"How are you feeling? What can I do for you?" I asked him. Kaspar seemed to have forgotten that he had called me to his room in the first place, but now that I was there, I did not want to encourage him by laughing. I was the adult in the room...kind of.

"Penis," he repeated, but this time more emphatically and with purpose. I tried, but ultimately failed to suppress a giggle this time. It was funny.

"Can I bring you anything right now, bud?" I asked again, ready to leave the room.

"Penis," he said once again, but this time it was with a bit more enthusiasm. Kaspar was saying "penis" to me now and not just at me. His eyes were now meeting mine. We were making a connection. A penis connection.

"Okay, Kaspar. Goodbye!" I responded, not knowing another way forward.

"Pee-niis," he replied, matching perfectly to the syllable the intonation of my goodbye.

Kaspar was not trying to brighten my day, but just by being his strange and wonderful self, he managed to do so anyway. The unpredictability of human behavior such as his is what sometimes makes this work so entertaining. I never know what awaits me in each room I am about to enter. It might be sad and horrifying. It might be hilarious and heartwarming. Sometimes, it is all those things.

MEET YOUR KIDS WHERE THEY ARE

I was the first person to ever shave her legs. It was a super intimate thing. She was about to become a teen, and she wanted to feel like everyone else. It felt like one of the nicest things I could have done for her.

- Amy, pediatric oncology nurse, mother

After more than a decade of working as a nurse, I am unable to recall every child with whom I have interacted. Too many children have passed through these halls and spent time in these rooms for my mind to hold on to all of them. The faces of children—even those whom I was once very familiar with—become hazy in my mind after a few years. At times, my recall for these kids is jolted only when I see their parents.

One morning, I walked into the room of a boy I was assigned to take care of. At first, I thought that we had never met before, but then I saw his mom and dad standing at his bedside. I instantly remembered those two worry-ridden yet determined expressions, those kind faces. They had been in the hospital a year prior with their son. Alberto was thirteen years old and suffering from a brain tumor. During that long stay, I had often been his nurse.

The progression of Alberto's disease since that time was remarkable but not surprising. The average survival time for Alberto's disease from diagnosis to death is less than a year. He had been sick now for close to two years. When I last saw him, he had already begun to suffer from the neurological impacts of his disease, but he was still able to interact. His speech was a bit slurred, but he could tell me what he needed. His limbs were weak and flaccid, but he could still shift his body with some help. He could reach out for his parents and for his sweet brother. He could smile then, too. He did that a lot, I remember.

Now though, Alberto was almost totally dependent on others—unable to turn on his own, hard of hearing, mostly blind, incapable of vocalizing, and diapered. His expression was stroke-like, and mostly a blank page.

He could no longer breathe easily either. He often gagged violently and gasped for air as he attempted to eject the thick secretions that slowly pooled in his airway. When this happened, Alberto's dad or I reached for the nearby suction device to manually purge what the boy could not. As we suctioned, we all stared at the monitor above the bed that indicated Alberto's current oxygenation status. The urgent and blinking number in flashing yellow would plunge into the low 70s, pause dramatically, and then slowly make its way to the cool blue of the mid 90s where we wanted it to be. The stress of not knowing when that number would rise again was too much.

Every time, I fought the urge to press the button on the wall that would send emergency help to the room. Every time, Alberto managed to recover. The tension in my body eased as Alberto, freed from his phlegmy burden, relaxed into slow, deep breaths, and his arched body sank back into his bed.

His parents, who unintentionally mimicked their son's body language, also descended back into their own tense bodies, remembering to breathe again as well. This repeated emotional and physical trauma put us all on edge and caused his mother to experience extreme anxiety. Over the course of the days during which I cared for Alberto, the uncertainty of his respiratory status was the only certainty.

During one quiet afternoon, the last day I took care of Alberto before he left the hospital and a few months before he died, he was sleeping calmly in his bed. The shades were drawn, the room dim. Alberto's father, who had been up all night watching his son, was huddled under a blanket on a nearby couch. Because Alberto was extremely hard of hearing, his parents were accustomed to screaming in his ear so that he would comprehend their words. After three days of hearing their kind but loud voices directed at their son, it now felt unusual to be present in this new hushed silence.

His mom and I were standing by Alberto's bed, watching him sleep. She was holding one of his contracted hands in both of hers, quietly recollecting to me the outgoing and enthusiastic person her son had once been—the school subjects at which he excelled, the sports he had thrived in, the dreams for the future he once held.

"He has never expressed any anger about his disease," she told me. "We are so proud of who our son has become."

Alberto's mom then glanced at the stethoscope around my neck with the many colorful bands wrapped around it. "Take this one too," she said, as she removed from her wrist the rubber green bracelet with her son's name embossed on it. "So you will always remember my brave son."

What struck me in that moment was not the understandable remorse Alberto's mother felt for all the wonderful things her son had once been, but rather the love and pride she felt for what he currently was. She wanted me to remember who Alberto was in that moment, not who he once was.

It occurred to me later that this kind of selflessness defines what it means to be a good parent. We as parents naturally hold so many dreams and expectations for our children, and we are often disappointed when they don't live up to the standards that we have arbitrarily set for them. Rather than expecting our children to be the people we wish them to be, it seems better to help them be their best selves in the place where they already are.

I think about this way of being a parent as I interact with my own kids. As a new father, I often felt it was my job to shape and mold my daughter's character to match my vision of what she should be, but it didn't work. Almost immediately, her strong will forced me into a cowed submission. My failures as a parent have been my best teacher.

These days, I feel much more comfortable just letting my kids be their weird selves. Sometimes, that means allowing them to get into iffy situations just so they can learn to find their way back out of them. Minor scrapes and bruises, bodies graffitied by semipermanent ink, small amounts of dirt ingested, and brains rendered slightly numb by too much cartoon watching are the most serious consequences of my free-range parenting. What my kids stand to gain, though, is a strong sense of self and an assurance that I love them for who they are, not what I want them to be. In any case, my kids deserve the chance to figure some things out for themselves, to develop at their own pace. This, I tell myself, is how they learn to be people.

Many years before I met Alberto, I was busy at work, bouncing between the rooms of kids I was taking care of that day. Around a corner, I encountered a young man named Mike in the hospital hallway. He was a skinny, pale teenager wearing a pair of thick dark-framed glasses that look much like my own. In addition to helping him see, these glasses served as a worthy stand-in for his conspicuously missing eyebrows. Mike had on a furry hat with a pair of fuzzy bear ears that made his head look much larger than it actually was. His shoulders were perched in a perpetual shrug, like twin crows roosting on top of his body.

When we crossed paths, he was standing in the middle of the hallway. Though we had never met before, it seemed as if he was waiting for me. It was clear to me then that Mike had heavy things weighing upon his mind, and he just happened to run into me first. He probably guessed that I, one of the few male nurses who work on this pediatric oncology floor, might be able to relate to his particular concerns. He was right about that.

Perhaps because the incident was fresh in his mind, or his sharing filter naturally low, he skipped the customary greeting expected between two people who have just met. The first words out of his mouth after a strangely familiar "Hey," described an incident, weeks earlier, in which he had tried, but failed, to masturbate into a cup in order to bank his sperm before his chemo treatment began. "It was way too much pressure," he confessed.

Then, in a near stream of consciousness, my new friend described how terrified he was of his brain tumor, of surgery, of being alone, and of being misunderstood. For the final act, his girlfriend had just broken up with him as well. Here he was, dealing with all the stress, sadness, and misgivings that are baseline with being a teenager, plus a goddamn cancer in his head. Then, on top of all that, we ask him to jerk off for us.

When he was done speaking, Mike's shoulders slunk down in tired defeat. His thin body sank down on a nearby window seat like a deflated balloon.

Before I could muster a reply, I was transported back to a time when I too was a teenager. I understood intimately all the emotions he was describing to me as if they were my own. If someone had asked teenage me to masturbate into a cup, I probably would have turned red and then fainted. No future children for me, regardless of if I had wanted them or not.

"I don't have cancer and I never have been in your exact situation," I told him. "But, I understand how you are feeling right now, how scary and isolating life can be. I understand where you are at. I was once there too."

Mike smiled back at me but said nothing. After so much talking, it seemed as if he had virtually run out of words. He pulled off the fuzzy bear hat, revealing a less fuzzy scalp. The chemotherapy had already stripped him of most of his hair, but he seemed to hold himself a little higher than when I first encountered him.

"Thanks, I have to go now. Bye," he blurted before he turned around and walked back to his hospital room.

I never saw Mike again. Like many of the kids we treat here, the bulk of his oncology treatment took place in the outpatient setting. I still think about him though. After he unleashed all his fears and emotions that day, my first inclination was to comfort him, to tell him that it would all get better for him eventually. But that was not a promise I could make. That was also not what he needed to hear. Instead, I hope that I was able to just meet him face-to-face in that turbulent emotional space he was inhabiting that afternoon—to really be present with what he was feeling—rather than expecting him to imagine a time in the future when it would all eventually be alright.

I thought about Alberto for a long time after he passed away, too. Of course, I was not wondering what he was doing with his life, but instead what it must have felt like to have been him before he died.

Then, one day, his parents came to visit the hospital. The occasion was Alberto's birthday. I imagine that it must have been very difficult for them to return to this place. Whenever Alberto had been here, it meant that his condition was deteriorating. Still, they came back to honor their son who had spent so much of his time at the hospital. I was not working that day, but I was touched when I heard that they asked about me. They wanted to see me and say hello. We had shared some very meaningful moments together.

Before they departed, they left photographs of their son to give to all the nurses who had once cared for him. The photo captured a moment when Alberto was still healthy, well before his disease changed his life forever. When I returned to work a few days later, I sat down with the photo of Alberto. In it, he has an enthusiastic smile on his face, a twinkle in his eye. He seems to be laughing knowingly about something outside of the frame.

The boy in the photo was not a person I recognized. I never met this Alberto, so full of life and happiness. Even in the small black-and-white portrait he was radiant. Sitting alone in the break room with that photograph in my hand, I felt a heavy sadness come over me. Some spare tears ran unheeded down my cheek.

Even so, I felt grateful to have known this boy during the latter part of his illness. That was an important part of his life too, a time when he was still growing and changing as a human, even though he was slowly dying. To have known Alberto before he became sick, I thought wistfully to myself, would have been something very special, though. Truly experiencing all he had to offer the world and the people in it was something I had missed out on.

YOU HAVE WHAT YOU THINK YOU NEED

What if their soul is still around? What if they are still there? They deserve to be treated with respect because that was their body.

– Kirsten, pediatric oncology nurse

During the first two years of my daughter's life, we spent an incredible amount of time together. We had our daily routine down pat: we had nowhere to go and all day to get there. We walked around our neighborhood, sometimes for hours. She cuddled against me in the carrier or sat upon my shoulders, grabbing my ears. With my ukulele in hand, I sang songs to her on a park bench overlooking the lake near our home. We rolled around on the grass near that lake and chased after the pigeons and geese, but never caught them.

On one slow and sunny Saturday morning, I cautiously asked my wife if it would be okay if our daughter and I officially became best friends. Even though it sounds silly, it was a serious question for me. I love my wife in ways that I surely do not always properly express, but my affection for my kids often overshadows that relationship.

This closeness to my children is an integral part of my identity as a person, but it is not an object I can physically hold or touch. It is an intangible predisposition that will always be a part of me, independent of where my children are, regardless of what they are doing. Even when I feel like the worst father in the world, this closeness remains a part of me. It is my salvation. I'm just not always aware of it.

In the hospital, too, parents are so accustomed to caring for their children that they are often not aware of their own intimate dependence upon them. They lose sight of it even though it is always around, guiding their thoughts and actions. Kirsten told me a story about a set of parents who, after losing their son, sought out something that they already possessed.

She wasn't there when their son, Leo, died and was brought to the morgue, but I was. I was Leo's nurse on his last day. I remember that his parents sat with his body for a long time. His mother was mostly silent as she sat by her deceased son. Leo's father was often wailing in sadness. He was angry too—at this injustice that nobody was able to fix or prevent. We always allow a grieving family to spend as much time with their child as they need. Some choose to leave quickly, while others can't bring themselves to leave their child for many hours.

There is no rule book for this type of situation, and during this time, a nurse is still assigned to take care of the patient. Leo's parents made impressions of his still-warm hand and foot in plaster, which is a common memento for parents who have lost a child. Eventually though, they left their son in the care of the nurses who knew him so well. When I brought him to the morgue with my colleague, Monica, Leo was still clutching his plastic Buzz Lightyear doll in his thin arms. To infinity and beyond...

Kirsten recounted that a couple hours after they had left, Leo's parents called to say they had forgotten the handprints and footprints that they had made with Leo when he died. They really wanted them, she told me. They would send someone the next day to get them. Kirsten and a few other nurses looked everywhere: in the room, in the garbage, but they were not to be found.

Kirsten and two other nurses, Leah and Dawn, made the uneasy decision to remake the prints. These simple items embodied the last memories that these parents had of their son. These objects made out of plaster mattered to them. Leo had just been brought down to the morgue a few hours before, so Kirsten and her nurse colleagues decided that they would go back there to try and make new prints for his family.

These three nurses went down to the morgue, slid Leo's body out from his container, and unzipped the white bag. There was nobody else around. The room was quiet except for the rotating hum of the refrigeration unit and their own human sounds echoing off of the stainless-steel walls. Kirsten and the other nurses were trying to make new handprints, but it was not going well. Rigor mortis had already begun to set into the boy's small body. The cool conditions of the morgue hadn't helped. His hands were locked into tight fists. His small body was rigid and inflexible.

Although the situation wasn't at all funny, there were moments when the nurses found themselves nervously laughing. Yet, they told Leo what they were doing, why they were doing it, and that they felt so bad about disturbing him. They apologized to him so many times as they stood him up in the curing plaster mold in order to try and preserve his footprints. The final result did not look good, but they all agreed that it was better than nothing. When they had done what they could, they cleaned him up, zipped that white bag shut, slid his body back into the cold unit, and left the room as if they had never been there.

"I couldn't believe what we were doing—mixing plaster in the morgue. This little guy. It felt ludicrous. Some people might think this was completely unnecessary, that it was totally weird, but at the time it felt really important for the family to have these things," recalled Kirsten.

There is a special place in my heart for Kirsten. She has mastered the art of being sweet while at the same time refusing to take anybody's shit. Kirsten's arms are heavily and fancifully tattooed, but at work, the floral designs are always covered by a long-sleeved shirt she wears under her scrubs. At some point during her routine night shift, her medium-length hair often finds itself piled into two pigtail buns on the top of her head.

As we talked, Kirsten's arms were crossed over her chest and she had a rather flat expression that belied a strong emotional reaction to a profound experience. Hearing this story in her sunny and eclectically decorated apartment, years after it occurred, it was not surprising to me that she did not once refer to Leo as what he actually was—a body. As she projected back upon this profound experience she always said "him" or "he." He was not an "it" to her. Her relationship with that "little guy" was present and real.

In my conversations with Kirsten, it was heartbreakingly clear to me that moments like this remain extremely personal to her. Her intimate understanding of the phenomena of death, pain, and love are not isolated from the work she does here. These experiences inform her thoughts and beliefs, but they rarely simplify them or explain them away. It is a process that is dynamic and sometimes cathartic, but not one that, for her at least, often leads to sure resolution or clear answers. What is unknowable remains that way. What Kirsten does know is that the bodies of these children—some whom she has loved and others whom she barely knew—remain sacred to her. That is enough.

The next day, Leo's family came back to the hospital to retrieve the remade plaster molds of their son's feet. They made no mention that these death prints were quite flawed, that they were different than what they recalled making when he had died, or that his handprints were not among what they received.

Ultimately, it seems, it is not the objects we acquire in order to remember our loved ones that matters, but rather the sheer intimacy and naked presence that goes into creating and giving these objects meaning. These parents already possessed what they had come back for. Their salvation—like mine—was with them all along. A parent's connection to their child will never disappear, even if that child's body does. The impressions of a hand or foot are merely echoes of the body that once pressed them. They do not contain all that the child once was or all that he will always be in his parents' minds and hearts.

BREAK FROM THE HEARTBREAK
LOVE IS BLIND

You know that your nurse coworkers get it. You don't even have to talk about why something is weird, important, or funny. They know.

– Kirsten, pediatric oncology nurse

Kids are rarely left alone in the hospital. Their parents, and often their siblings, are present to support and love them. For this reason, we practice family-centered nursing. We adapt our care to improve the well-being of both the child and their family. Although it is often challenging for nurses to navigate multiple needs and personalities in one room, it is worth the trouble. Making the whole family happier benefits everyone.

Emily, a nurse who I have worked with for a long time, told me the story of a particularly unique family who was always together. Their young daughter suffered from retinoblastoma, a rare form of cancer that develops from cells in the eye. Surgeons had removed her affected eye, leaving her half-blind.

She was not alone in the dark, though. Both her mother and father were fully blind since birth. The only member of the family with unfettered sight was the girl's infant brother, who was seemingly forever strapped to his dad's back. Between the four family members, they had three seeing eyes. Despite their limitations, though, they seemed to get around just fine.

Blindness does not ensure courtesy, however. The girl's father was known to be a bit rude and hard to work with at times, so Emily was prepared for some attitude when she entered the room that day.

She was leaning down over her young patient with her back to the father when he said roughly, "Leave it!" Before Emily could respond to his strange order, he commanded her to "SIT!" even more sternly.

Then, Emily felt the father's warm, moist breath on the back of her neck. She whipped around with the intention of confronting him, only to find a dopey-looking Labrador staring her in the face. It was the family's seeing eye dog. The girl's father, sensing that his four-legged guide was encroaching on Emily's space, had been attempting to reign him in.

"Come, boy," the father requested of the dog once again. "Leave that nice nurse alone now."

In some patient rooms, even the dog is part of the family.

MAGICAL THINKING–IT WORKS UNTIL IT DOESN'T

I was dumbfounded when he died...I forgot he was going to die.

– Jess, patient care assistant, baby whisperer

Despite how much I enjoy being a dad, there are times when I wish it was less complicated, not as hard, and certainly more fun. When both my kids are losing their minds in unison and fighting over who can be more obnoxious, I sometimes conjure an entirely alternate reality in my mind to escape what is happening in front of me. Here, I usually still have kids (though not always), but they are perfectly behaved, and they always listen. Somehow, I am perfect too. This creative self-delusion rarely lasts long. The blood-curdling cries of my progeny interrupt my dissociative fantasies like a pesky alarm clock.

Still, no matter how many times this fantasy of ease is dismantled, I always return to it. I simply can't help but think magically at times. If I can't change reality, perhaps I can transform it into a new and more pleasant shape. It is comforting for me to believe that some small action I take may alter the course of my child's distressing behavior at any given moment. It is equally illogical for me to snap and yell at my children and believe that my outburst will somehow be effective at enacting change, but I still do it.

I have been guilty of this same kind of magical thinking many times during my career as a nurse. It happens involuntarily, perhaps in order to protect my own emotions and sometimes simply so I can make it to the end of the day without losing my mind.

When I was a new nurse, a young boy I was taking care of had a massive and unexpected seizure in the middle of the night. As he convulsed before me, I could not bring myself to hit the emergency button that would have summoned a cavalry of nurses and doctors. Instead, I yelled at one of my nurse colleagues outside of the room for help. It was the exact wrong thing to do. In that moment, I irrationally hoped that by not pressing that white button I would prevent it from becoming a serious situation. Despite my inexperienced handling of the incident, the boy was just fine.

On another day, a small boy was quietly sitting cross-legged in his bed, watching television while absentmindedly playing with his toy monster truck. In that moment, a weakened blood vessel in his brain ruptured and caused him to bleed inside his head. His nurse, witnessing the surreal and pained change that came over his face, immediately slammed the button on the wall that sets a code in motion.

A faceless voice alerted the entire hospital via loudspeaker, "Pediatric BMT, Room 6, Code White. Pediatric BMT, Room 6, Code White. Pediatric BMT, Room 6, Code White."

Within a few minutes, his room was overflowing with doctors, nurses, respiratory therapists, and pharmacists, working to save his life. The chaotic and disheveled state of his room afterward spoke to the urgency of the moment. Hastily opened emergency supplies were left lying on the floor. Linen torn from the bed to better expose a small, obtunded body was now piled in the corner. No matter how calmly and professionally a code is run, when it is over it often looks like a tornado had touched down. The space of the room also felt larger because the boy and his bed had been taken away. His small toy truck, which had been knocked under the hospital bed, sat isolated in the middle of the room.

From the corner of the room, where she stood shakily, his mother had watched the entire resuscitation and emergency transfer of her son. She had a strange smile on her face. I'll never forget that expression, which was so incongruent with the scene before her. It seemed to me then, that much like the time when I failed to press that white emergency button on the wall, she too was willing for it to not be true.

Faced with such morbid possibilities in the hospital, all of us here—patients, loved ones, even the professional caretakers— at times try to shoo away what is happening in front of us. Many parents in the hospital have shared with me their own personal form of magical thinking, hoping that they can change fate by willing or forcing it away. One mom told me that she routinely pleaded to the universe to cure her son of his disease.

She told me through tears one day, "I would have conversations in my head in which I vowed to be a better person, just don't take my kid from me. I'll change whatever you want me to change."

Susan, Ari's mom, was all too familiar with cancer and other diseases. She was not naive about death. Despite this, she told me that she often thought to herself, I am doing such good work. I will get a pass. She found comfort in her self-deception that the universe would reward her for her own kindness and protect her son. It was an improbable bargain with the universe—that by compassionately caring for those who were dying, she could somehow avoid a similar fate with her own children. Years later, as she cared for her own very sick son, she told me that fate spoke back to her in her mind. You are gonna learn your lesson about the way things are, it told her.

I, too, have made the same bargain. There's no way my kids can get cancer. I am a pediatric oncology nurse, dammit. It would be too ironic, I have thought so many times. The bargain sounds fair, but it does not work. No matter how urgently I might will it to be so, there is no shield I can wield, no talisman I can hold, and no deal I can strike that would render my own kids safer than others. Irony is a mental construct that reality most often does not heed.

In the depths of her sadness and her frustration over her son's fate, Susan eventually let go of her quest to twist fate into curing her son. If she couldn't save him, perhaps she and the world could go with him. Maybe we'll be lucky and there will be an asteroid. We'll all die together, she thought to herself. "I was ready for a tsunami or maybe a plane to go down," she admitted to me.

Steven, a young man who navigated two separate bone marrow transplants to cure his aggressive form of leukemia, employed his own brand of magical thinking.

"I took on the Iron Man persona," he recalled about the self-made, resourceful, and brilliant fictional Marvel superhero. "In my mind, I would put on the iron mask and suit, and just kick ass. That's the way I looked at it, from the time of diagnosis to the end. I just had to put on that armor and do what had to be done."

It was a mask he needed to don often, if only in his mind, in order to cope with his harrowing circumstances. Steven was told that the chance of even finding a suitable donor was quite small. Over the course of many months, he endured physical and emotional punishments that would be difficult for me to fathom if I had not witnessed them myself. At his lowest, he experienced weeks of delirium and hallucinations, making it difficult for him to distinguish between sleep and awake.

One night, he felt something itching deep in his throat and, believing it was a blood clot from his ever-bleeding nose, he reached down and pulled out this long chunk of tissue. It was part of the lining of his esophagus. His brother, at his bedside that evening, still has nightmares about that moment. I was present that night too. As I regarded the pink, wrinkled piece of flesh that Steven had extricated from his throat, I too felt the need to imagine it away.

All that time, from diagnosis to eventual remission, Iron Man became Steven's guide through which he personified his thoughts and actions.

"The times when my body went septic were pretty wild. My breathing became shallower. My body felt weak. I was shutting down. I had to find every ounce of what was left to pull through. I had to be Tony Stark in those times. I had to be Iron Man," he told me.

To this day, Steven still looks back fondly and with a kind of nonchalant reverence at the manner in which he was able to frame his difficult experiences through the guise of a fictional character he so admired. I don't think he gives himself enough credit though. Steven's magical thinking helped to motivate and encourage him, but it would have been useless if not for his own strength of character. Steven is a survivor. It was his unshakable positive attitude and unique ability to look on the bright side of life that was most responsible for the brave face he showed his disease. It is the reason he is so successful in what he desires to be now: an advocate and mentor to other young people with cancer. Steven was always an Iron Man—he just didn't realize it.

Before Rylan died, he and his parents watched every Golden State Warriors basketball game while in the hospital together—his parents from a small couch, and Rylan from his little court, bouncing around and shooting jump shots in time with Steph Curry.

Rylan was on his third relapse from a very aggressive form of leukemia. I knew that despite his positive attitude, he was fighting an uphill battle. However, when witnessing moments of familial bliss like this, I was almost able to forget the real reason why these three people were living in this cramped hospital room together. It was not to watch basketball. They were here to save this boy's life.

The Warriors began that season with an epic winning streak and, in my mind, I conflated their success on the court with Rylan's survival. If the Warriors win, Rylan will live, I thought to myself. Simple. This was one of the ways I coped with what, for me, was a very scary reality—losing a person I truly cared about. Rylan was more than just a patient to me. From the moment I met him, I wished for his happiness and well-being in a manner that far surpassed my role as his nurse.

Every time the Warriors blew another team out of the water and increased their winning streak to what would ultimately be twenty-four games, I felt more assured that Rylan too would win against his cancer that I had envisioned as a hungry beast that wanted nothing less than this boy's life.

When Golden State finally lost to the Milwaukee Bucks in early December, I felt in my heart like Rylan had lost too. I knew intellectually that the two things were unconnected, but my emotions did not respect logic.

That evening, I was depressed and downtrodden. Even though Rylan was still very much alive—he would soon be on his way to the National Institutes of Health (NIH) for experimental treatment—some part of me was already mourning him.

Three months later, Rylan's doctors at the NIH told his parents that their son was in remission from his leukemia for the fourth time. Even so, his body had been through too much. A few short hours later, Rylan passed away while his parents were away from his bedside for a short time. There was nothing that could have been done to prevent Rylan's death. He did everything that was asked of him and more during his short and beautiful life, always with a smile. His parents too, went to the ends of the earth for their son. No amount of medicine or magical thinking could change how it ended up.

Eventually, the bleakest truth—that we and those we love may suffer and will die—proves unavoidable, despite our best efforts to evade it. Where magical thinking ends, though, something else begins. Parents who lose a child find a way to continue on, even as they grieve over the body of their dead child. Although it may take hours—days even—the rhythms of our most ancient clocks, our bodies, take over and lead us away from the inertia of sitting with our dead.

One nurse, Amy, told me, "The person has left, and you are devastated, but the fact that the world doesn't stop is the one thing that helps you move on. I think the body helps too. Eventually, you will be thirsty again. You will need water. In these rooms where everyone is very, very sad, someone eventually will say, 'I will be right back,' or 'I have to pee,' or 'I'm really hungry.' Your body does not let you completely stop, and the world certainly doesn't either."

GRIEF AND PAIN ARE PART OF PARENTING

That is when my grieving started—the understanding that my life is never going to be what I thought it would be. We were hoping for more time, but our life was different now. I think that when your child dies, grieving is for the rest of your life because with every life event, every milestone, they were supposed to be there.

— Susan, Ari's mom, hospice nurse

Loss is part of life. I have come to accept that the resulting grief is an inextricable part of my experience as a parent too. With my kids, I encounter such losses in miniature all the time, even though I am often too distracted to be fully aware of them. Each precious phase of my son's and my daughter's childhood is a time that I know will one day end. For my kids, it is a milestone they have achieved, something lost or gained, but for me it is a time I will never experience through them again. If having kids represents an opportunity for parents to vicariously relive youth through their child's new experiences, it is also another chance to experience loss when those times are gone—to grieve for them.

When my son finally grew some teeth, I was so happy for the experiences he would have with them—the new things he might eat, the clever things he might eventually say, the other mouths he might one day kiss, but I also secretly mourned the loss of that drooly, toothless grin. His goofy smile was transformed. It was gone forever and, strangely, that mundane reality brought me to tears.

Parents who have lost a child know a grief much greater than this. It defines them. It is a constant companion that eclipses all the small and quiet moments they once enjoyed or took for granted. Over a year after her son Ari died in her arms, Susan's grief had not yet subsided. If anything, it was deeper and more profound.

One day, as she neared the front of the supermarket checkout line, she recognized the man working there and she immediately froze alongside her cart of groceries. He knew my son, she thought.

"You look familiar to me," he said with a friendly smile as he scanned her items. "Oh! That's right. Our sons went to elementary school together. How many kids do you have now?"

"Well, I've got two," answered Susan curtly even though Ari, her oldest child, had been dead for almost a year.

"Oh wow, how old are they? What are they up to?" He was kind, but completely oblivious to Susan's discomfort, her mounting tension. She had avoided going to the market for over six months after Ari's death simply to circumvent interactions just like this one. Even now, it was difficult for her to tell people without crying that Ari was gone. Susan thought it was easier when the person questioning her about her children was a stranger—someone she would never see again—but this man had known Ari. It felt wrong to her to lie about his death.

"Twenty-six and twenty-four years old." She heard herself answering the man's question anyway. "My daughter is a musician. My son is an engineer." She couldn't say the words My son died. Not that day. She paid for her groceries and left the store. Susan was still in deep grief.

This kind of grief, this hurt, must feel like an ocean—unending, with murky waters that hit our human shores in waves that are unpredictable in their strength, direction, and character. From my experience, grief does not show up just when a parent loses their child. Rather, it is often present from the moment of diagnosis. Parents grieve for the loss of innocence and for a childhood cut short. They may grieve the loss of their child's hair, which they once put in pigtails each morning before school. No matter how good the prognosis is and how well their child does, there is always a loss to mourn that becomes bigger than ourselves.

I know about one family whose grief process was so intense that, even as their young son Avery still lived and fought his disease, his parents made plans to commit suicide together should he pass away. They were very open with the nurses and doctors about their intentions.

On one day when Avery's condition was particularly bad, his father told Kate, a nurse who often took care of his son, "He can't die. He's going to do great things in this world. He can't die." As she looked into his worried, bloodshot eyes, Kate did not doubt that these parents would follow through on their plan.

"They had so many dreams for him. They would have done it," Kate said.

Throughout Avery's illness, his parents put both his life and their lives on hold. It was always just the three of them in the room. They did not allow visitors other than their nurses and their doctors. They did not celebrate any holidays during their long hospital stay—not even Avery's birthday. Their behavior reminded me of when people sit Shiva, a Jewish tradition in which mourners take an almost complete break from the routines and involvements of everyday life. In that tradition, the loved ones focus on the memory of their beloved in order to honor them.

These two parents were mourning the loss of a boy still living—his childhood temporarily interrupted by the circumstances of his treatment and his parents' desire for him to just be a normal kid. Their torment over their son's situation was so great that they essentially said goodbye to the world in almost every way until he could once again fully be part of it. Fortunately, that day came for him. Avery miraculously got better. His parents' resolve was never tested by tragedy.

Although I have seen that caring for a sick child is extremely challenging for parents, this burden is certainly preferable to the alternative—life without their child. Many parents of deceased children long to return to a time when they possessed the singular purpose of caring for them. Parents who have muscled through this intense experience only to lose their children in the end often don't know what to do with themselves when they no longer have a sick child to focus their energy on.

Susan described it perfectly: "The grief part is really different than the part I went through with Ari when he was sick. It was easier going through that feeling then because he was still with me. In a way, I had a reason to be better. What is really hard now is seeing a future without Ari. When he was here, I did pretty good."

Another mother, Jaclyn, told me of her strong desire to be back at the hospital fighting cancer with her son, Ben. "I miss you, and all of the nurses and doctors, and being there, and that period of time when Ben was fighting cancer. I was with him every day, and we were assuming such a different outcome," she wrote me once.

When a child dies, their parents lose a part of themselves. Jaclyn wrote, "My body and mind think that [Ben] is still coming back. I have dreams about him most nights and I think constantly about him...that's maybe how it will be for a while."

I can relate to this ineffable longing. Like Jaclyn, I have come to depend on my children in a way I cannot readily put into words. They are simply part of me and, at the same time, something totally different and new—something better than me. If they were taken from me, I know I would long for them like these two moms long for their sons. I would miss their bodies inhabiting my space, their sounds reverberating in my ears. I, too, might willingly revisit the daily pain of it all being slowly taken away in order to temporarily reclaim that precious time.

Jason, Rylan's father, struggles with a different kind of emotional and temporal dislocation after the death of his son. It is his own very personal form of grief.

"I replay the moment he passed in my head all the time. That's never going to go away," he told me. "We are always going to grieve for him. We are always going to think of him. It is going to be like that for our entire lives. I don't want to stop thinking about him...I will sit there and talk with him like he is here. We drive by the cemetery all the time on the way to our house, and when I do, I always say, 'Hey buddy! What's going on?' like he's there, but sometimes I talk about him like he is gone."

Jason and Krisi told me that it helps them to be able to still communicate with Rylan even though he is not physically with them. Because of their strong faith, he is still a part of their family, still an older brother to the sibling he never met, and still an incredibly important part of their lives. They often have conversations with Rylan and can hear what he would have said in return.

Jason continued: "Just because he is not here doesn't mean that we aren't his parents. Some parents struggle with that. We are his parents. You can't just erase that."

I too have silently spoken to Rylan after his death, and I have found comfort in this one-way conversation. I know I am not alone among nurses who knew Rylan and still feel a strong personal connection to him long after his passing. Rylan was ebullient, with an emotional intelligence that rivals most grown people I know. He was mature beyond his years, even while maintaining the cheerful innocence of a child. We nurses were his best friends, and like friends do, he also offered support and affirmation in generous and unselfconscious ways. In talking to me, Krisi recounted that when they first learned of one of Rylan's many relapses, he could see that she was sad.

"It's okay mom. I will beat it again. I'll just do it," he reassured her with a knowing smile.

Thinking about Rylan now, I still miss so much about him. I miss playing basketball with him in his room—Justin Timberlake tunes playing in the background and his parents giggling from the couch, so happy to see their child having fun with his friend. I miss being able to make Rylan laugh by being silly and observing the natural ease of this surprisingly actualized individual.

I used to call to him from the bathroom of his hospital room pretending to be his toilet. With an exaggerated, muppet-like voice, which was my version of what a toilet would sound like if it could talk, I would say "Rylan, Rylan...I need your poop." It was a joke that a five-year-old boy and a forty-year-old nurse with questionable humor could appreciate in equal measure. Rylan would fall giggling to the floor.

I also miss witnessing Rylan performing acts of kindness without regard for himself. It made me want to be better too. His sweet altruism sometimes came in the form of unexpected compliments.

He once told his nurse Allie as she performed a delicate procedure, "You're doing a really good job. I'm doing a good job by staying still, but you're really doing a good job." Another time, late into the night, he called a nurse to his room and asked her to help a crying baby who was in the next room over.

Mostly, though, I struggle knowing that there is a person as exceptional as him, who is no longer sharing the world I inhabit. That will never seem right to me. In some of my more fanciful moments, I have imagined that Rylan was cured of his leukemia and years later, as a young adult, visits me in the hospital. I picture him looking around the familiar hospital halls—a place he once navigated breathlessly while dressed in his well-worn Spiderman costume, his parents lagging behind him. I see him revisiting the room he once spent so many months in: Room 13. I see him playfully tracing with the toe of his shoe the spot where his mini basketball half-court was laid out in tape all those many years before.

The young boy I knew never had more than a sprinkle of peach fuzz upon his scalp—I used to love rubbing it when I saw him—and his skin always seemed impossibly pale, almost translucent. In my musings though, teenage Rylan has grown tall and put on weight. His skin is ruddy, and his face has matured into the form and visage of his father. His hair is reddish and cut short. His glasses are perched on the end of his nose, like his dad's. Rylan's toothy and loving smile is just the same as I remember it to be. When I greet him with a feigned handshake that quickly morphs into a bear hug, I feel his smile beaming over my shoulder. We both have tears in our eyes, but they are tears of joy. I would give so much for this dream to come true, but it never will.

At work, there used to be a binder at the main nursing station, and inside of it was a lonely piece of paper with two columns of names. Under the first column were the names of nurses who had chosen not to be notified of a patient's death. Under the second column were nurses who did desire to be called at home when a patient they loved had died.

A nurse who agreed to such a notification could be anywhere when the news came their way—relaxing at the beach on a Sunday or watching an old movie at home. The choice to either diminish or increase the space between our work and our personal lives says a great deal about how each nurse deals with their feelings for these children.

When I have received that call notifying me that a young person I have known and cared for has died, I often don't know how or what to feel, but I do not question my decision to be informed. I can hear myself saying tonelessly back into the phone, "Thanks for letting me know," but I don't actually know if I truly am thankful for it. After I put the phone down, I often sit silently for a long moment of stunned remembrance and respect. Then, after a helpless sigh, I continue what I was doing before I heard the news. I don't know what else to do. I don't know how else to be. I can't lose myself every time someone I care about dies. It happens too often.

As we all encounter these small daily losses and seek shelter from the storm of the greater ones, we distract ourselves by looking to the future and by reminiscing about the past. Susan told me that she still remembers walking Ari to kindergarten on his very first day of school, and how it felt to her.

"I dropped him off and I was so sad," she lamented as tears began to run down her face, even though the event happened over twenty years earlier. "I felt this hole in my stomach because now he was going to school. Now, I think back to the way he felt inside me when I was pregnant, when I was carrying him. I couldn't see him, but I felt him. I felt his being. I feel Ari's presence a lot now. I feel like he goes through the day with me. Some days I don't feel him and I get sad. I ask him for help if I am about to do something scary. I didn't know about that part—that you have a relationship with the person for the rest of your life, even if they are not there physically."

As they left the hospital for the last time and it was clear that Ari did not have much time left to live, his mom told me that her ever-optimistic son was still looking toward the future. He sent a text to a close friend of his that read, *Things look really bad. I might only have 6 months left.* It was an optimistic prediction from a boy who often chose to look on the bright side of a dark time. Ari died two weeks later. He took his last breath as the night transitioned into a new morning. When he died, it was just him and his mom, alone together like they had so often been before.

"I think," said Susan, as we sat together in her living room, "I think that he wanted to die with just me there. I didn't think about calling his sister and father. Selfishly, for me, I didn't want to take care of them too. I just wanted to be with my son."

Not long before he died, during a time when he was still feeling well enough to appreciate the little things, Ari exclaimed to Susan, "What an adventure we are having! Some people go through their whole lives and never have a relationship like this."

Susan will always grieve for the loss of her dear boy. That is the price she must pay for having the good fortune of being his mom for twenty-six years. Though she still grieves for Ari, she will never feel that she didn't do enough for him in his time of need. She will never blame herself for not spending enough time with or caring enough for the boy she raised, loved, and watched die. Susan will never, not for one second, think to herself that her son didn't know how much she loved him. Ari knew it. We all did, too.

BREAK FROM THE HEARTBREAK
CANDY IS DANDY

Our work is so inappropriate. Everybody is inappropriate. There is always something to laugh about.

- Allie, pediatric oncology nurse

I remember a thirteen-year-old patient I cared for when I was a very new nurse. A tumor located right next to his pituitary gland had caused him to gain a massive amount of weight, so he appeared much older than he actually was. It was only his high-pitched voice, pimply face, and general childlike manner that gave away his age.

His name was Daniel, and he was very sweet. He enjoyed his sweets too; the medication he was taking gave him a tremendous appetite. He snacked constantly in his hospital bed at all hours of the day and night. His large stomach was like a picnic table. His multiple chins were like pillowy steps that led up to his loveable, pudgy face. This human dining surface was scattered with the remaining crumbs and wrappers of candy and various salty treats.

Because Daniel was so large and weak, he couldn't move around much. We helped shift his large form as often as we could in order to prevent him from developing pressure ulcers on his expansive body.

One evening, as another nurse and I moved Daniel onto his side in order to inspect the skin on his back, we noticed five brightly colored marks on the boy's skin. Upon closer inspection, we discovered much to our delight (and also our horror) that the blemishes were not bruises, but peanut M&Ms pressed deeply into Daniel's pliable and spongy skin. The source had obviously been one of Daniel's snack breaks gone awry. As we regarded this strange site, one of the half-melted candies, giving way to sweat and gravity, dropped to the bed. It left behind the faint but discernible yellowish ghost mark of its recent sugar-coated tenant.

It was difficult not to smile at this sight and at the knowledge that Daniel had unknowingly disproved the long-touted promise by the folks at Mars Chocolate that M&Ms melt only in your mouth. In my head, I rewrote the famous jingle that had planted itself in my consciousness as a child: The milk chocolate melts in your mouth, not on your [Daniel's] back.

Daniel was receiving palliative care when I knew him, and he died not too long after that day we found the candy pressed into his back. His fate was so sad and unfair, but fortunately that is not all I remember of him. Although I did not know him terribly well, I will never forget his sweet disposition and the sincere, loving way he gazed at his mom over his thick glasses.

Of course, I will also never forget that chocolatey discovery we made upon his backside. The memory of it still makes me smile, and a little bit hungry for a sugary snack.

LET YOUR KIDS TELL YOU WHAT THEY NEED

He wanted so badly to keep going for his family...He needed to hear that his parents would be okay.

– Amy, pediatric oncology nurse, mother

"Papa, can I tell you something?"

My daughter often asks me this question when she wants something and wants me to want it as much as she does. Sometimes, the want feels so big and scary to her that she can only whisper it in my ear, lest the universe hear it and somehow deny her. She doesn't quite know how to whisper though. She cups her small hands around my ear like a megaphone. Her warm kid breath and excited inhalations usher in an only slightly softened version of her normal inside voice. I listen and experience a cherished but almost unbearable tickling sensation as she elucidates her childhood desires into my brain.

Of course, there are so many things that I want for my kids as well. Things that I, too, can only whisper to myself in fear that the universe will not provide. Things that they do not necessarily want for themselves. It is a constant challenge to do right by my children while not forever imposing my own parental will upon them. The experience of parenthood is one forever stuck between a rock and a hard place, of not wanting what I need and of needing what I do not want.

I once heard a seasoned nurse ask the father of a lethargic and dying teenager, "Have you told him that he can let go if he wants to, that you will be okay?"

At the time, I was shocked by her bold and straightforward question to this hyper-attentive father. I was a new nurse at the time and had yet to experience much death. I didn't know that kids will often hold on to their lives long past their desire to live if they feel that their parents are not ready for them to go. Some children need permission to tell their parents what they truly need.

That conversation resonated with me for a long time, mostly because the concept puzzled me. I could not comprehend a desire to die because I had not yet witnessed real pain. Most children have the innate desire to please and protect their parents. I would not truly understand that until I had kids of my own. Children need to feel safe and secure to express their needs, especially when they know those desires are not shared by the people who love them the most.

Lukas was a teenager who had leukemia. He was gentle and soft-spoken. His favorite color was purple, and he loved to cook. As he waited out the days, weeks, and months in the hospital, he found refuge in fantasy video games. He played the role of the mystical warrior-wizard who vanquished evil creatures with his spells.

Playing his video games—where he controlled the elements of ice, fire, and earth—brought him comfort in an otherwise sterile hospital setting. I often walked into his room to see his robed character blasting fireballs at giant winged dragons that were attacking him on the big TV screen attached to the wall. To me, these evil video game creatures seemed like a thinly veiled metaphor for the leukemia that also was attacking Lukas relentlessly. I asked him to tell me about the game he spent so much time escaping into and he told me excitedly and in great detail about the world where his character battled.

I was also in Lukas's room the day his primary doctor told him that despite the heavy doses of chemotherapy he had received in the months prior, the disease was still in his body and would not be going away. His mother stood by him, her hand upon his shoulder. She had not been expecting this news that day.

This kind and experienced doctor offered the possibility of different therapies that might work, but he also was quite honest that further interventions might only provide Lukas more time—most of it being very sick in the hospital. Lukas took the news quietly. I don't think it surprised him.

The doctor and I then left Lukas and his mother so that they could absorb the news together. Not long after that discussion, Lukas declined any further treatment. He did so with the full support of both his parents, who always considered his welfare above their own heartache. Even though they would have gladly held on to their boy for as long as possible, they knew he didn't want to be in the hospital. They knew he felt tortured there. They did not want him to die in such a place.

The bad news Lukas received had, in its own way, been a gift of clarity for the kind of life he wanted to lead with the time he had left. He would not have been able to actualize this profound choice without his parents' help. Instead of reacting to their own pain and fear, they listened to him. They gave him a voice.

Before Lukas left the hospital to die at home, he told one of his most trusted caregivers, Jess, "This is not living. This is not where people are supposed to be. I belong in the woods with the bugs and the trees and the molds. I want to be swimming naked in the river and barefoot in the sand. This is not normal."

That was one of the most honest statements that I have ever

heard in my life. Lukas's sensitivity to his environment and the way in which he chose to inhabit his world was so insightful and brave. He had figured out something that often takes many people a lifetime to realize—how he truly wished to spend his time on this earth. Not all patients choose the same path as Lukas did. Many kids and their parents feel compelled to hold on to their lives as long as possible. Some, knowing their pain can be better controlled in the hospital, choose to remain there. They don't feel like they belong in the world outside the hospital any longer.

Lukas died a few months later. I was told that his last months were what he wanted them to be. He was at home with his family, his friends, and his pets. His bare feet touched the sand on the banks of a river; his naked body felt its cool, living waters.

GIVE YOUR KIDS THE TRUTH
THEY ASK FOR

I want to die. I am tired of doing this, but I want you to use my body to do an autopsy and figure out this cancer so other kids don't have to go through it.

– A six-year-old boy with leukemia

As the muffled sounds of public radio vibrated between my skull and the walls of the kitchen, I wondered exactly how early in the morning it was. It was dark outside, and the display on the microwave provided no clue, just a scrolling entreaty for someone, anyone, to **PRESS START**. Contemplating the implications of this digital plea, I longed for a button that would start me in a way my twice-reheated coffee had not. In its absence, I stared blankly at the wall in front of me.

The paint was peeling off in places where leaned-back chairs had pressed into it. The fading splatter of a mango smoothie, like evidence at the murder scene of tropical fruit, pointed a guilty finger at my three-year-old sitting on her knees across from me. She was quite awake and looking deceptively innocent as she hummed to herself between slurps of cereal. A serpentine trail of milk dripped down one side of her face and onto the floor.

"Papa, PAPA! I don't want you to die," she pleaded suddenly into her bowl of Cheerios.

"Do you know what it means to die?" I asked reflexively.

"To go gone."

I was awake now and surprised by her succinct grasp of the

concept. This was not the first time my daughter had brought up a topic that is difficult to talk about. When she does, I've always tried to be honest with her. I don't know if this is the right thing to do. I usually parent from the hip and, to me, it doesn't feel right to lie to my kids. Even though death was a topic that I should be uniquely qualified to talk about with her, I felt nervous that I would say the wrong thing. I did not know if my familiarity with people dying should be hers too.

"Are you going to die, Papa?" she asked.

"Yes, love. Someday, I will die."

"Oh," she said, followed by a frown and more slurping. I was grateful that she sounded disappointed. "Papa, Papa...I don't want to die too. Do I have to, Papa?"

"Yes, baby. It happens to all of us," I replied gently. "But it won't happen to you for a long time."

"Because I'm just a niña?" she asked.

"Yes, my niña," I laughed, "Finish your cereal. We have to get ready for school now."

A few weeks after that philosophical discussion at the breakfast table, I sat with a thirteen-year-old boy in his hospital room. Sebastian was lying inert yet very alert in his bed. He had been so sick for so long that he could not even turn his body on his own. He was alone. I had not seen his family in weeks. Even though he was playing a video game and mostly ignoring me, he didn't want me to leave.

"Hang out with me, David," he said. And I did. I had spent so much time with this kid over the course of his long stay in the hospital that I was almost as used to him as I am to my own kids. When he was overwhelmed with pain, loneliness, or frustration in his quiet hospital room, he asked for me. We had that kind of relationship.

"Have you ever seen a ghost here?" he inquired, still staring at the video screen in front of him.

"A ghost? Hmmm. I've seen some strange, unexplainable things, but I'm not sure about a ghost. I have heard stories from people who think they've seen ghosts here though. If there were to be ghosts anywhere, Sebastian, I imagine it would be in a place like this," I answered.

Instantly, I regretted my candid response and the existential can of worms that it might have opened for this boy.

"Do kids die here?" Sebastian then asked me. I was surprised by his naivety.

"Yes, Sebastian, they do," I said.

"What ages are they when they die?"

"A lot of different ages."

"Are they sometimes my age, David?"

Sebastian was no longer distracted by the video game in front of him. He was looking directly at me. The muscle-bound Viking character he had been controlling in his video game stood in place too, surveying his strange alien world while huffing up and down. Somehow, the Viking also seemed to be waiting for my response. As I considered what to say next, I noticed the dry trail of a bloody tear drop that had dripped from Sebastian's hemorrhagic eye earlier that morning.

"Yes, your age too, Sebastian," I said reluctantly. The room was silent for a few heavy moments.

"That sucks," he said with a curious half-smile, which I had come to both count on and adore. Buoyed by Sebastian's brashness, I agreed with him.

"It really does suck, Sebastian."

We both went quiet for a while. Seemingly unfazed, Sebastian turned his attention back to his game. His Viking avatar continued his quest to kill goblins or whatever creatures inhabited the digital alien world.

I took a deep breath and just sat there. My hands were shaking. As with my daughter, I did not know if my answers had been helpful to Sebastian. Even though he had responded blithely to what I said, I was sure he was still rolling about the implications of our discussion in his mind. I wanted to be able to talk honestly with Sebastian about all the questions he had, even if my answers were difficult for him to hear. I desperately wanted to answer all these questions for myself too, even as I began to consider that those very questions might not be the right ones for me to be asking.

I've often asked myself: Why? Why couldn't we help Lukas beat his cancer? Why did Rylan get told he was in remission for a fourth time only to die an hour later while his parents were having lunch? Why was Sebastian slowly fading away before my eyes? Why not my daughter or my son? Why all this suffering? Why? Why?

The longer I spend doing this work and observing just about every possible outcome—children who go on to live full and healthy lives, children who are cured only to return to the hospital years later, children who die after long and painful battles with cancer, and those who die quickly without pain—the fewer convincing answers I have, the less truth I find.

Being truthful with my kids means more to me than just answering their questions honestly. It means helping them ask the questions that serve them best, even when they don't always appreciate the answers they discover. For myself, too, I've come to accept that there will be no way forward for me if I continue to perform the same unresolvable interrogation of an unfair world. In order to thrive in a place where people dear to me die despite our every intervention, I have undergone an emotional and intellectual reorientation. I have stopped asking Why? because that question no longer serves me.

These days, I ask instead: How? How can these kids live their best lives? How can I play a role in that process? How do I continue this work and still grow as a person? How do I parent my children as I see how cruel this world can be to them? How? How?

We may not cure every child of their cancer, but each of us can help make those moments in between more precious and full of life. For me, that means remaining present with the pain and the joy. It means being honest with myself and with others. It means always trying to find humor and lightness in places that seem so goddamned dark. These are ways I can have control as a parent and as a nurse without giving in to despair, ways I can have a positive impact without fooling myself that I can change reality. This refocus does not suggest that I am giving up and relenting to fate. I want all these kids to be cured, and I want my own kids to live long and happy lives. I will be helpful in whatever part of that process that I can be.

Changing my attention to the manner in which I do this work, rather than regarding it as being completely outcome-oriented, has become a life preserver for me in the hospital. It has changed how I feel and act at home too. Every moment spent with my children seems to present a thousand different decisions or actions I might take. There are times as a parent when I say and do the wrong thing, times when patient inaction would serve me far better. However, rather than attribute my many mistakes to my shortcomings as a father, I now see them as an opportunity to be a better one in the future, to be fully present with my kids rather than be fully in charge of them. Failure is inevitable, but how I react to it is my choice alone.

There are times when my actions are not true to this idealistic attitude. As a father, I still lose my temper and later beat myself up over it. At work too, watching a child suffer in pain has its way of deftly short-circuiting even my most well-thought-out intentions. On one particularly hard day at the hospital in which every entrance to any of my patient's rooms felt like a fresh heartbreak, I began to feel, in despair, that there was no point to this work at all.

"This is not my life. These are not my kids. My kids are healthy," I admitted to Ashley, a coworker I feel close to. The words were harsher than I intended them to sound, no matter how true they felt in the moment. The expression on my friend's face was concerned. I don't think she had ever seen me so downtrodden, so raw.

My life at home and my life in the hospital are different worlds, but they will never be completely separate for me. My feelings as a nurse to these sick children will always inform the choices I make and the hopes I hold as a papa to my own kids. I will never possess the superpower of complete compartmentalization between nursing and parenting.

I realize, too, that Nurse Papa, the perfect parental superhero I have imagined into reality and strived to emulate, simply does not exist in the way I thought he might. Nurse Papa is human, not superhuman, and even though he has good intentions, he is fallible. He is just doing his best. When his best is not enough, there is almost always another chance to get it right. I've had to give up on the quest to be perfect. Honestly, I don't even know what perfection means to me anymore. I might not recognize it if it were standing right in front of me.

In this bumbling process called parenthood, my kids have

become my most honest guides. Just by being themselves, they reveal the truths I ask for as well as many that I do not. They each teach me lessons that I would otherwise never have learned or even asked. My daughter's insatiable curiosity forces me to answer questions for which I really have no satisfactory explanations—to imagine improbable worlds in which her great-grandmother and a dead spider go to the same place after they die. I have no idea where that place is or if it exists for either of them, but my daughter implores me to describe it in detail anyway.

"Tell me a story, Papa!" she consistently demands, and the force of her truth-seeking becomes its own magic. She routinely points out little gems of life that I would never have noticed—a tiny snail resting on a green leaf, a single vibrant pink flower high in the bows of an otherwise-naked tree.

My son's constant smile and reliable good nature remind me not to take every setback in life so seriously, to relax when I can. He runs, head down, toward all of life's possibilities without worrying about what awaits him around the corner. Sometimes he falls, but he always gets right back up and continues on. I have learned from both of these wise children that, as their dad, there will be shitty times and there will be amazing times, and I may often be puzzled about the difference between the two. Nothing ever stays the same. This parent circle just keeps spinning around, and I can't just hop off when the way it wobbles displeases me. I would not want to if I could.

On yet another early morning at home, when my brain was once again brimming with sleep even though my body was awake, I sat back and watched as my two half-naked children laughed, danced, and wrestled together. We were going to be late for school, but I could not summon the energy to care about that. The kitchen—

their improvised stage—was an absolute mess, and they were making it messier, but I couldn't bring myself to pick up a broom or wash a dish. I was content, rather, to remain a hands-off observer to the chaotic glee of my kids.

Whatever they were creating in front of me seemed worthy of my patience and full attention. As they danced without rhythm to a song playing on the radio and fell giggling to the floor, I laughed out loud—a rough cackle that made me feel a bit lightheaded. All the while, and barely aware of it, I silently intoned a near-constant mantra of appreciation. It played out in my mind like the soundtrack to a seamless and perfectly repetitive movie, one I could easily watch forever. Thank you for my beautifully healthy children. Thank you that I get to see it...all of it.

The dance party and my meditation upon it ended abruptly as my youngest child butted his head against his sister's knee and began to cry hysterically. As my boy stumbled into my arms, the last bars of the radio tune hummed sweetly in the background, overtaken now by the cries of an upset toddler.

BREAK FROM THE HEARTBREAK
ONE LAST LAUGH

I just farted...sorry...just had to warn you.

– Corianna, in the medication room

Corianna, my ever-so-funny friend and coworker, once told me that her only motivation for coming to work was knowing that something or someone would cause her to "laugh her ass off." More often than not, Corianna was the source of that laughter for all of us. Although she spoke in jest—no army could have kept her away from these bald kids she loved so much—her theory never needed to be tested. Even among all the sadness that occurs here, there is always something to smile or laugh about.

Not too long ago, one parent, whom I had not formally met, asked me, in what seemed to be complete earnestness, if he should call me "Liz" or "Elizabeth." He was responding to the white board on the wall in his son's room upon which each nurse writes their name at the beginning of their shift. I had forgotten to erase the name of Elizabeth, the previous nurse, and was rewarded handsomely in laughter for my oversight.

I responded to him with an equally straight face, "You can just call me David. Liz is my stage name. Thanks for asking though."

I wish I could have told Corianna about that moment, if only to see that familiar naughty look in her eyes and the way she would physically lean against a wall when something was just too funny for her to remain standing. She would have slapped her thigh in an exaggerated motion and exclaimed, "O-M-G, David."

I never got the chance to tell Corianna that silly story and so many other things she would have laughed at and cried about. She died a few months before that funny moment happened. Unlike the very sick patients we care for every day, her death was not one I was prepared for, or could have ever predicted.

Nurses, more than any other group of people, are accustomed to encountering death and pain. Although we are affected by the suffering of others, our job calls for a measure of detachment, the ability to move forward without faltering. We carry this unique sensibility into our personal lives too. The traumas we experience are sometimes compartmentalized because, in the hospital, that is a helpful device to make it through a hard shift and a challenging career. Habituated to hurt in general, nurses will admit regrettable tales of not bringing their own children to the E.R. for wounds and ailments that nonmedical parents would consider quite urgent.

When Corianna died, many of us grappled with how to confront our own personal grief over the loss of our friend and mentor. I have found no clear prescription for how to best experience sadness while still moving on from it. I do believe, though, that Corianna would want us all to keep on laughing, even as we cried.

When my friend Stephanie called to give me the news that Corianna had died, I was at the airport, struggling to manage too much luggage and two tired kids. I could hear the strain in Stephanie's voice before she said that Corianna was dead—she and Cor were besties—and when she finally got the words out, I did not believe her. I thought it was a strange, but funny, Corianna-endorsed joke.

Corianna was such an amazingly generous person. More than anybody I have ever known, she would have wanted the people who loved her to remember the joy that was her life, rather than the sadness that was her passing. It is a choice how we feel about these things.

Sometimes, it is possible to find sincere joy and levity in the face of hard times. It is the perspective of the struggle that serves us most and helps us to grow, despite the pain it brings along with it. In other moments, though, the right choice is to feel sad or depressed, and that's just fine as well. Sadness does not always have to be fixed. Corianna taught me that more than anything—that it's important to honor how you feel rather than judge it.

Since Corianna died, I think of her often. There are many little things that remind me of her in the hospital on a daily basis. Her name inevitably comes up in a funny story someone tells. I find myself staring at the empty corner of the med room where she and I once had an important exchange that ended in a belly laugh and a hug. I glance at her delicate cursive signature that still graces a patient's admission card. Her name there indicates that she was one of the sweet girl's primary nurses. My name, in messy block letters, is written on that same card as well. It feels good to have our names so close to each other, to be part of that same club of care and affection. I feel lifted up by Cor, still, even though she is gone.

During those moments at work when I am sad, scared, or unsure, I often ask myself: What would Cor do? How would she make this better? If I take the time to listen to my slow-beating heart or pay attention to my steady inhalations, in and out, I sometimes find the answer I am seeking. I hear Cor's soothing voice, with its muted Southern accent, in my mind. Even though Corianna is gone, she has never really left.

These days, I feel differently within my relationships with many of my nurse colleagues. It is a closer and more aware experience. The loss of Corianna has a lot to do with that. She taught me to embrace my true self, to honor that person. Over the last decade, I have seen so many of my friends at work in emotionally vulnerable places; I, too, have allowed them to view me in this way, without artifice. In this place, where we all experience such intense moments, this relationship with the people I work with has been a life preserver as well as a beacon that guides me. Now, I simply hold on tighter to that feeling of closeness. I don't want to lose it. I need it to keep moving forward.

I have learned from my time here, and all the people who have shared it with me, that although life does often end here in the hospital, it never stops. The wheels still turn, albeit on a bumpier road and with perhaps a less-certain driver at the helm. Those same experiences that people take for granted in the outside world—things that bring both pleasure and pain—continue here too. They take on a special resonance and meaning that add to the bittersweetness of it. All of it is a part of our day.

ANGELO AND HIS HUMMINGBIRD
THE END

Right before she died, she said that she really wanted to go to the beach and fly away. I think that was her four-year-old way of saying goodbye.

- Amy, pediatric oncology nurse, mother

"David. It's good to see you. Come in. Come say hi to Angelo," were the welcoming words from Dana, Angelo's mom. He was just four years old. The last two years of that short life had been spent in and out of the hospital as he received treatment for a brain tumor that never had much chance of being cured. On this last visit, though, he was here to die. I was here to say goodbye.

I had known this boy and his family since they first came to us. I had seen them change and evolve as they encountered their son's disease. In that time, I too had changed as a person. I was a new, often-fumbling father of one when I first met Angelo and his family.

Now, a few years later, I had two young kids. I was still fumbling, but I had come to see that as part of my journey as a dad. I was more secure in my lack of control over who my children were—and who I was. Much of that newfound maturity was learned from the examples set by the parents of the kids I care for at work (through their strength, their love, their patience, their humility, their horrible losses). Parents like Angelo had.

I had also matured greatly as a nurse. I felt more relaxed and centered than when I first began nursing so many years before. Paul, Angelo's father, had once said to me kindly, "David, thank you. You've taught us so much," as I prepared them to go home, months before this final return to the hospital.

"Are you kidding me, Paul? You are the ones who taught me," I replied, so humbled. "The love you two give to Angelo and your family is an inspiration to me. You are the kind of parents I hope to be to my own kids." We were both teary and not hiding it.

Angelo, the boy now lying in bed before me, was different than the child I remembered. His legs were longer, and he had aged out of the pudgy, round face of a toddler. He was a little boy. Most strikingly, Angelo had a full head of straight brown hair, a physical feature I had not seen on him for almost two years.

He was surrounded by three generations of family: his older sister, his two parents, and his grandparents. Although each of them was grieving and coping in their own way, the space was not heavy or depressing. On the contrary, the mood of the room was light and inclusive. Dana and Paul had always welcomed people who cared about them and their son to visit his hospital room. Even as he was dying, this warmth had not waned.

At one point, a hummingbird hovered, somewhat magically, right outside the window to Angelo's hospital room. It would stick around for many minutes, dart away for a while, but eventually return to its previous post, surveying the room and the boy on the other side of the glass.

"It's Angelo's grandmother, I think," remarked Dana. "She's watching over him, over us."

I placed my hand gently on Angelo's cheek. It was pale and mottled, but still warm to my touch. He was sleeping and seemed comfortable. Suddenly, I felt awkward as I stood there over him.

With my hand still touching Angelo's face, I turned to his parents. "I don't know what to say," I stuttered honestly, through stray tears. "You are all so special. You are such amazing parents. Angelo is so...I'm so sorry." What I wanted to say was Angelo is so lucky, which even now seems like such an odd thing to think about a dying boy, but it was true. He had great parents.

"It's okay, David. We know," said Dana. She understood. She hugged me.

Later that day, Angelo's condition changed in ways we expected it would. His breathing became labored and agonal. There were long, unnatural gaps of time between each wheezy inhalation. His coloring became greyer and more mottled, too. His skin was cool to the touch. This is how a child dies.

In an unexpected and quiet moment, Angelo sat up suddenly, startled but with eyes tightly closed, and took a labored breath. His skin was now a dusky-blue color.

Corianna was at his bedside in that moment, helping as she always did. She always knew how to read people. She knew the truth they needed to hear. "Pick him up. Hold him. It's okay," she said to Dana.

Dana, who was thirty-eight weeks pregnant at the time, climbed up into the bed with her son. "Do you want me to hold you? Do you want to die in my arms? Do you want to lie next to your baby sister?" she implored of her son.

Angelo's limp form was draped across his mom's large belly. His unborn baby sister, whom Angelo would never meet, but whom he already loved dearly, was pushed up right next to him as he continued to gasp for air—a neurological response communicated from a dying brainstem.

Gasp. His little body tensed.

"We love you, Angelo. We are so proud of you. It's okay to go," said his mom. Paul hugged her from behind and put his hand on his son's forehead.

Gasp, another minute later.

"Just let go, just let go. It's okay, my love, just go."

Gasp, yet again.

"We're gonna be okay. I know you want to meet your baby sister, but you are always going to be part of this family. You are going to watch over her. Just let go."

She was still holding Angelo gently but firmly to her belly. He continued to take labored breaths, and then he would not breathe again for as long as a minute, sometimes even longer.

Between weak inspirations, his tiny body would relax, motionless and silent for what felt like an eternity. At one such time, Kate, the calm and present nurse caring for him, gingerly put her stethoscope to his chest to check if he was still breathing. Just as she paused to listen to him—holding her own breath—Angelo took a giant gasping inhalation.

Kate jumped back in surprise, vocalized an astonished yelp, and everybody in the room, including Dana, began laughing. Angelo had played his last trick on his last nurse.

"You just scared your nurse, Angelo!" Dana was smiling through heavy tears. "Just let go, Angelo, come on son, please let go."

Not long after that tragic yet surprisingly comic moment, Angelo took his last gasp. A few minutes after the final breath of his only son, Paul bolted to the bathroom and vomited violently into the toilet. A week later, Dana went to another hospital near their home and gave birth to Angelo's little sister.

Up until the very last moments of Angelo's life, Paul and Dana were doing what they did best—being his parents. Their hearts were always open. Their deep grief, their joy for the gentle life their son had led, and their nervous anticipation for the new life that would soon join them was as beautiful as it was complicated. This was their son. This was their family. This was their life.

A few weeks after Angelo died, I was strolling with my sleeping son around the large lake near our home. After an hour of vigorous sandbox play in the park, he was snoozing soundly in his stroller with his head nodded over to one side. His face and hands were sticky and stained a crimson red from a bag of ripe cherries we had devoured together—his eating methods being less precise than mine.

Tired more in my mind than in my body, I found a place on a nearby bench and just sat for a while, surveying the environs of this very peaceful, urban setting. Groups of migrating birds—geese, pelicans, and many species I could not identify—flew around and filled the soundscape with various honks, squawks, and tweets.

Every few minutes, the same group of frenetic pigeons would spontaneously launch into the sky in one bunched-up group, fly around in a seemingly random trajectory, and then return once again to their former spot. While I'm sure there is a reason for this, like many other natural phenomena, I am ignorant to it. They act just like some people I know, I thought smugly to myself.

Just then, a hummingbird darted right up to me like a tiny, feathered bullet train and dexterously alighted on the handle of my sleeping son's stroller. I rarely see these birds at rest, and I could not take my eyes off it. The patch of feathers on its head and neck were a startling array of reds, purples, and oranges that seemed to undulate in and reflect the light of the bright sun above.

"Hello, Angelo," I said to the bird, fully expecting a reply. It did not answer back, but continued to perch there quietly, its long nectar-sucking beak still pointed in my general direction. "Maybe you are Angelo's grandmother? How is he?" I asked, feeling a bit foolish, yet willing to believe in a world where wild animals can talk and also inhabit the souls of the people we once loved.

Just as I was about to continue my silly part of this one-sided conversation, perhaps to dig deeper into the general phenomena of soul translocation and other ineffable topics, the beautiful bird suddenly ejected from its post, leaving me and my wonders behind.

"Goodbye," I said to the empty space in front of me. "It was good to see you."

EPILOGUE
CAR TALK

Forget about it, Papa. Just, forget about it.

- my daughter, comic relief, and mini Tony Soprano

"So Papa..." my now four-year-old daughter opened up the conversation as we drove home from school one day. "...Papa. Let's talk about the ways how a person can die, Papa."

She was sitting strapped into her car seat, her little legs kicking rhythmically into the back of mine. Next to my daughter was her little brother. He was gazing distractedly outside the window with his ever-present thumb taking up valuable real estate in his mouth. Our car inched slowly along the freeway off-ramp next to our home. Traffic. This conversation was happening no matter what.

"I'll go first, Papa. One way you can die is by falling in a plane like the Bamba man. He fell from a plane, Papa, he did," she assured me. She was referring to Richie Valens, of course, the famed singer of the song "La Bamba." A while back, we had listened to that song over and over again, and I recall that moment as being one of the first times she asked me about death. "Is he alive, Papa? Or is he dead, Papa?" she had asked me innocently.

I don't know for sure what about that particular song made her so curious about the mortality of the singer, but I suspect it is Valen's singing voice. Even though, at first listen, "La Bamba" sounds celebratory, there is a subtle folklore sadness to Valen's tone—it is somehow mournful. My daughter, always observant and aware, except when I am asking her to do something, had picked up on that sad quality. She is canny like that, mindful and attentive.

I do have a pretty good idea what I am in store for, trying to raise this acutely curious and slightly eccentric person I have the pleasure of calling my daughter. She will never be easy, but she will always be interesting. She will always challenge me to be the best and most present father I can be. As her papa, there is absolutely no way to phone in parenthood. It is an unruly and raucous circus in which I will forever be that acrobat, way up high on the tightrope, shaking and just trying to keep my balance. It will undoubtedly take some finesse to raise this child without falling.

Translated into English (which you really should never do; it ruins the song), the lyrics of "La Bamba" describe my experience of parenthood rather well:

> *To dance the Bamba,*
> *To dance the Bamba,*
> *One needs a bit of grace.*
> *A bit of grace for me, for you,*
> *Now come on, come on.*

To be a good parent to your children—whether they are sick or healthy, silly or serious, tragic or comic, dead or alive—requires a bit of grace. Parenthood asks you to do and say so many things that may not come naturally, things that may actually scare you into learning something about yourself that you were not expecting to discover.

I never understood that until I had kids of my own—that my words, thoughts, and actions as a parent would truly reveal the kind of person I am inside. Before my children entered my life, I thought I knew exactly who that person was, but I was so wrong. He is an altogether different human being whom I have had to become acquainted with. He is one whom I have not always been proud to be—definitely not—but for the most part, he has always been true.

When the day is done, my kids are fast asleep in their beds, and I am once again lying on that too-small couch with my lovely partner, being true might just be good enough.

THANK YOU FOR READING
NURSE PAPA

Please consider posting a rating or a review. Reviews not only help other readers find books, but they also let readers know which books may end up their new favorite!

ACKNOWLEDGEMENTS

Writing *Nurse Papa* has been a labor of love, and I could not have done it without the help of so many people. The process of writing this book has rarely been an easy or straightforward journey for me. I started with an idea and a drive to tell the stories of the brave patients I have cared for, their families, and also my dedicated colleagues. You all allowed me into your lives and gifted me with your honest and poignant perspectives. Thank you for placing your faith in me to tell your stories. You have become my most patient teachers in love, parenting, family, and so much more. My life and indeed this book is so much more meaningful with your contributions.

I'd like to thank the very early readers of *Nurse Papa*: Heena Shah, your astute insights about what *Nurse Papa* was and what it could be were invaluable to my early writing process. Kaveena Singh, my intrepid wife, you patiently read this book in all its many iterations and were refreshingly honest about its shortcomings and also its potential. You then talked me off the emotional ledge when I mistakenly felt that there was no way forward. I could not have done this without you. Keith Metzger, my older brother, you read *Nurse Papa* with the keen attention of a scientist. You also taught me more than I ever wanted to know about the correct usage of 'which' and 'that,' for which I am forever grateful.

This book could not have been written without the support of my parents Bill and Kathy Metzger, who taught me the value of caring for others by doing just that themselves for so many years. I followed both of you into the medical profession and I am forever grateful for your support and advice. And to my younger brother, Adam Metzger, you were always there with a helpful thought and a not so gentle kick in the butt when I needed it.

Thank you to my many friends and fellow writers, who listened to me, read early chapters, gave me encouragement, and allowed me to bounce ideas off of you. You know who you are.

I would also like to thank the GenZ Publishing team for believing in this book when nobody else would. The subject matter of *Nurse Papa* can at times be difficult to encounter and I am ever appreciative of your efforts to introduce it to a mainstream audience. Erika Skorstad and Destinee Thom, my GenZ editors, you invested your time and energy into making *Nurse Papa* better than when you received it and for that I am so very appreciative.

Finally, I could not have written this book without my two kids, Dayus Rahki and Szivika Kaur. You two are just the best. You have changed my life for the better in absolutely every single way. I only hope that I can be a father and a human worthy of your respect and love. Now, please, just go to bed. It's late.

ABOUT THE AUTHOR

DAVID METZGER, R.N. has worked as a pediatric oncology nurse at UCSF Children's Hospital for his entire nursing career. The bravery, laughter, perseverance, and the many smiles of the children and their parents who he has helped care for have been the inspiration for this book.

David's inspiration in life and art is his wife Kaveena, an asylum attorney with the soul and skill of a master chef, and his two adorable kids, Szivika and Dayus, who are still figuring out what they are passionate about.

David is also the host of the popular *Nurse Papa* podcast. In each episode, Nurse Papa takes a deep dive into a story of parenthood and comes out on the other side with a better understanding of what makes kids and their parents tick. You will laugh, you will cry, and you will learn more about yourself with each episode.

ABOUT THE PUBLISHER

GENZ PUBLISHING is on a mission to bring new authors to the world.

It can be nearly impossible for writers with promising talent to be recognized in the publishing and digital media industry. There are many unheard voices in the publishing world because of the often costly (for time, energy, and money) requirements for breaking into it.

Since there often seems to be an under-representation of new and innovative voices in the publishing world, we decided it was time for change.

GenZ Publishing emphasizes new, emerging, young and underrepresented authors. We're not a vanity press. Instead, we're a traditional, indie publisher that focuses on mentoring authors through each step of the publishing process and beyond: editing, writing sequels, cover design, marketing, PR, and even getting agented for future works. We love to see our authors succeed both with the books they publish with us and with their other publications. That's why we call it the "GenZ Family."

OTHER GENZ NONFICTION YOU MAY ENJOY

It's Not Goodbye, It's See You Later by Richard L. Belford

I Went, I Saw, I Shared by Pam Canington

Out by Scott McGlynn

Made in the USA
Las Vegas, NV
19 May 2022

49095116R00121